CALIGULA FOR PRESIDENT

BY THE SAME AUTHOR

Colors Insulting to Nature

A Massive Swelling: Celebrity Re-Examined as a Grotesque, Crippling Disease

CALIGULA
FOR PRESIDENT

Better American Living Through Tyranny

Cintra Wilson

BLOOMSBURY

Published by Bloomsbury USA, New York

All papers used by Bloomsbury USA are natural, recyclable products made from wood grown in well-managed forests. The manufacturing processes conform to the environmental regulations of the country of origin.

LIBRARY OF CONGRESS CATALOGING-IN-PUBLICATION DATA

Wilson, Cintra.
Caligula for president: better American living through tyranny / Cintra Wilson.—1st U.S. ed.
p. cm.
ISBN-13: 978-1-59691-588-6 (pbk.)
ISBN-10: 1-59691-588-9 (pbk.)
1. Caligula, Emperor of Rome, 12–41—Fiction.
2. Presidential candidates—Fiction. I. Title.

PS3573 . I45685C35 2008
813' .54—dc22
2008024622

First U.S. Edition 2008

1 3 5 7 9 10 8 6 4 2

Typeset by Westchester Book Group
Printed in the United States of America by
Quebecor World Fairfield

For Batman

The world has no importance—once a man
realizes that, he wins his freedom.
—Albert Camus, *Caligula*

CONTENTS

INTRODUCTION: A NOTE FROM YOUR FUTURE DIVINELY ELECTED, SUPREME EMPEROR IN CHIEF
xvii

A NOTE ON TRANSLATION FROM THE COAUTHOR
xxvii

1. HELLO, I'M RULING CLASS, AND YOU'RE NOT: LESSONS MY IMPERIAL DYNASTY TAUGHT ME
1

2. HOW TO WIN FRIENDS AND INFLUENCE HISTORY; OR, HOW I LEARNED TO STOP WORRYING AND LOVE DOMESTIC PROPAGANDA
17

3. THE REALITY CRISIS: MANAGING YOUR CONSENT AND MANUFACTURING YOUR PERCEPTIONS FOR PROFIT AND PROFIT
36

4. DIVUS CALIGULUS:
NEO-CAESAROPAPISM, AMERICAN STYLE
53

5. A DEMOCRACY BY ANY OTHER NAME
WOULD STILL BE THE OLDEST, MOST
CLASSIC EXCUSE FOR BEATING YOU
UP AND TAKING YOUR STUFF
77

6. I AM THE WORD, THE LIGHT, THE SUN
GOD AND THE LIZARD KING; OR, PLAUSIBLE
DENIABILITY—THE REPUBLIC DOES NOT
RECALL
93

7. THE ECONOMY: READY TO LOOT
WITH THE BIG DOGS
110

8. BUILDING AMERICA'S DREAM-GULAG:
HOMELAND SECURITY AND THE ART OF
SUPPRESSING SLAVE REVOLTS
144

9. A HELLO TO ARMS; OR, ETERNAL
WAR FOR ETERNAL WAR; OR, CATCHING
YOUR DICK IN THE ZIPPER OF IMPERIAL
OVERREACH
174

10. THE POLITICAL ANIMAL MUST EAT ITSELF: PARANOIA, CANNIBALISM AND EXISTENTIAL ANGST
200

ACKNOWLEDGMENTS
219

SOURCES
221

Hearts. Minds.

CALIGULA©®™∞

won't sleep until he has yours.

THE MOST POWERFUL NAME IN LEADERSHIP FOR OVER 2,000 YEARS.©®™∞

Caligula©®™∞ is a global leadership brand, presenting and promoting unique leadership products to **corporate, professional and consumer nations** around the world.

Caligula©®™∞ is committed to **executing key leadership needs**, placing an unrelenting focus on strategic surveillance, security, **mind control** and reconstruction services that span the complete range of global **disciplinary** sectors, with a proven track record of success tackling core issues, public crises, **emergency** execution, issues **obfuscation**, reputation control, religious superiority and a pervasive media presence.

Our innovative strategic **rigor** uniquely positions us to identify and mobilize the Caligula©®™∞ brand to address issues anywhere in the world, with memorable **commercial** results.

A passion for leading today's new commercial government environment.©®™∞

As a nepotistic relations leader, Caligula©®™∞ and the Caligula©®™∞ brand family are recognized and respected in sovereign markets worldwide for **providing** powerful, divine, **leadership-based solutions** to **dominating** academics and industry professionals in the fields of **energy**, **defense**, media, law, financial services, scientific research, beauty, **incarceration,** telecommunications, health care, **space** colonization and high **fashion**.

Leadership is responsibility.©®™∞

Caligula©®™∞ cares about the impact Caligula©®™∞ leadership products inflict on the people and places touched by our mission. A lot.

From jet engines to **arbitrage**, oil refineries to offshore financial services, medical crises to custom state-building, Caligula©®™∞ supporters worldwide have the imagination, energy, culture capital, **armaments**, connections and long reach to **enforce uninterrupted access to the powers a superpower craves.**

CALIGULA©®™∞

Everything your nation needs to rule the world.©®™∞

INTRODUCTION: A NOTE FROM YOUR FUTURE DIVINELY ELECTED, SUPREME EMPEROR IN CHIEF

Ave!

I'm Gaius Julius Caesar Augustus Germanicus—better known by my fans as Caligula. (I am called "Zeus," in the bedroom, but never mind.)

Like Rome in its third act before total collapse, twenty-first-century America seems to be in a self-destructive tailspin.

Look at yourselves.

If you're like most Americans, you are a depressed, isolated consumer. Lonely and restless, with no community efforts to dignify your time on Earth, you work too hard (if you're even employed) for meager wages toward unspecific goals you will never personally benefit from. Your small and hopeless life can only be dignified through the purchase of new technological gadgets, "It" handbags, plasma TVs, plastic surgery and other large-ticket luxury items, on credit. You drink too much, you're addicted to porn and you're deeply, perhaps irretrievably, in debt (due to the magical fiscal thinking that you'll somehow be making exponentially more money in the future than you ever have before).

As a nation, you're burning through your natural resources and your borrowed money as if there were no tomorrow, because in some lemming-like way, you collectively fear there might not be one.

And there are people who have organized this thinking of yours, and people who have benefited greatly from your suffering.

(I confess: I'm one of them. Guilty!)

To medicate yourself away from any real awareness of your own powerlessness and/or the discomfort and anxiety it makes you feel, you engorge yourself on wild excesses of prescription drugs, fatty foods, simulated violence, and wet-brain-feverish entertainment.

In your weakness and confusion—stricken by the paralyzing fear of your own wretched impotence that both fuels your fear of terrorism and stokes your desire for a strong national paterfamilias at the head of the big table—you have allowed your executive branch of government to become perfectly, beautifully, legally imperial.

These recent corruptions are nothing new, really—au contraire. They are as old and impenetrable as a mummified nun.

My point is, America is *thisssclose*—right on the forty-yard line—of having a real, live, old-fashioned, dynastic totalitarian monarchy–cum–military dictatorship. And I intend to drop-kick America orgasmically through this goalpost.

I never really liked this country, but things are just

starting to ferment enough to get interesting here. I'm feeling quite at home.

I can tell you from experience: This kind of "Armageddon cometh" behavior is a self-fulfilling prophecy.

Your empire has peaked, the corruption recently tattooed in place will be very difficult to laser off—and, indeed, the next executive in charge will have no personal incentive whatsoever to erase these inherited perks and extrajudicial magic powers.

Take the doctrine of Unitary Executive Theory, for example—a fantastically obscurantist loophole-stretch so diabolically luscious it really should be renamed the Project for a New American Mussolini. This gem argues that the president possesses all the executive power and is therefore above all regulation, oversight or supervision . . . and that Congress and all other annoyances that seek to check and/or balance this new paradigm of brazen executive dictatorship can feel free, while they're down there, to shine the Holy Presidentio papal pimp-boots.

Then there's dozens of crazy-sexy-extralegal presidential directives—National Security Presidential Directives (NSPDs) and Homeland Security Presidential Directives (HSPDs)—created under insanely top-secret Cones of Silence and Veils of Mystery. Since these entirely lawlike bonus-extras relate to national security (because we are, after all, under a grave and constant threat of terrorist acts that will make 9/11 look like Shirley Temple doing ballet on the back of a miniature pony), about two thirds of these are so massively classified that you won't even have the foggiest idea what they are for at least twelve years, and maybe never . . . but you can, however, possibly be prosecuted under them.

Boy, times have really changed. When Charles I tried to pull the same stunt on his Parliament, the English wasted no time assembling an impromptu platform at the Banqueting House in Whitehall and gleefully sawing his head off.

Who'd have thought that Americans would be such gutless, nippy-wipe fifi-bags about these things, compared to the *British*?

Don't tell me . . . I guess you're all expecting to receive this letter in the mail from your next president (since you've probably figured out by now that you won't be receiving another largesse of three hundred to six hundred dollars in tax rebates):

My Fellow Americans:

There are some indescribably wonderful legal implements left over from the last administration that give me a ridiculous amount of totally uncheckable executive superpowers that make me, personally, the most powerful human being on the planet. I just wanted you to know that even though you, the American people, have no sophisticated idea what these deep-dish legal documents actually say or mean, I am voluntarily taking all the sexy, power-granting parts out of them and rendering them null and void. I am so incredibly decent, I know I oughtn't trust myself with so much Godlike, abusable, consequence-free authority.

By the way, while I'm at it? I am going to give up sugar, butter, oral sodomy and Vicodin. Because it's the right thing to do.

Leading by example,
Your Loving President

Do not hold your breath next to your mailbox.

There's only one hope for America to return to any kind of cleanliness and political purity: the total disgrace of a brutally insane and psychopathic dictatorship, which will finally rile enough sufficient outrage among the American populace to slice out the current body politic like a diseased gallbladder.

This job has my name on it ☺.

This is why I recently realized that I am the rightful Holy Emperor of the United States.

Here's my campaign platform:

You think it's been bad lately?
Ha ha ha ha ha ha.
Oh, mirth. I just wet my bespoke toga.
I'm not laughing *at* you! I think you're *adorable*.
It can get SO-O-O-O—O-O-O much worse.

I pledge to remove all obscurantism and mystery from the process of leadership. No pussyfooting around the ring, no debates, no superdelegates.

I vow to kidnap my opponents and extraordinary rendition all my most visible dissidents to undisclosed CIA black-site dungeons, to serve as examples. I vow to tilt all the banks into cowering submission with my own sovereign funding arm, and I will *personally* terrorize all members of the Senate who oppose me with snakes, blackmail, witchcraft, extortion and other threats until they are gibbering, weepy and compliant.

Your whole "empire" has been run by rank amateurs so far. Wrought with failures of will. But I vow to abuse my authority to the fullest extent of my lavishly psychotic imperial imagination.

Resistance to my hostile takeover of the democratic process is futile. (Actually, truth be known, the whole "democratic process" thing is kind of quaint and outdated, like the Geneva Convention, or burying Vestal Virgins alive in the Evil Fields near the Colline Gate in times of national crisis.)

My leadership is a stark inevitability.

The Caligula brand is just the topless mermaid carved on the iceberg I am about to ram into the hull of your great country.

I am major academic research perverted to meet my own needs. I am the telecomopoly that spies on you, the major network television news station and its local affiliates and newspapers that present domestic propaganda as fact, and thirty-three premium cable channels that sedate you with gunplay and tits. I am the pharmaceutical giant that sells you both illness and cure, and your self-abusing mortgage and financial service that predatorily lends to itself and then faints into the waiting arms of sovereign-wealth funds. I knit my own guns, tanks, bombs and aircraft. I am private intelligence service corporations, scads of private equity, and a saucy little escort service–cum–sushi bar on K Street. My Praetorian Guard is jacked to the stud-beams on state-of-the-art implements of mass death. My offshore assets alone are enough to ensure my rule and that of my descendants for the next four thousand years. (I'd love to elaborate, but then we'd have to discuss certain operations that would endanger national security. In other words: I'd tell you, but then I'd have to shoot you, ha ha ha.)

And I have jails, jails, jails, jails, jails. More than enough for you and your family, and your family's families, and their future children. Forever.

I'm the new kind of corporate brand.

I have recently enslaved both Uncle Ben and Aunt Jemima. I raped Betty Crocker in front of the Pillsbury Doughboy and am now using his corpse as a waterproof throw pillow in my wet sauna. Of course, I am speaking metaphorically, but that is only because I am also about to become your religion.

In summary, I make the research that makes the news that makes the wars that make the entertainment that makes the public opinion that sells the wars that dictate the votes that make the laws that sell the weapons and the drugs all over the world. Olé.

Actually, Russia, China, Exxon, Wal-Mart and the House of Saud and I all dwarf-tossed over you, and I won. Yes, I cheated.

Bow down and tremble.

Like a real, grown-up imperial leader, I have nepotism, divinity and corporate synergy on my side. You've already been trained not to resist: Your womb-to-tomb consent has already been manufactured by Madison Avenue television psychiatrists, whose bold thought-leadership ensured that you have been imprinted with slavish loyalties to our brands since you were six months old.

You hadn't a chance, darlings: We had you at Barbie.

But there is hope: It's called *total submission.*

You may have some doubts about me, due to the negative buzz that has been surrounding my name for the last eighteen hundred years or so.

You might be asking yourself: What can Gaius Caligula, a blood-drunk, epileptic, sister-molesting, transvestite Sun God and sharklike Machiavellian superbrand, do for me and my fellow Americans?

More to the point: Will Caligula detain me in prison indefinitely until I am finally given pellets of angel dust and led blindfolded into RFK Stadium to fight hyenas wearing nothing but a loincloth made of ham?

You don't need to worry about that right now.

Concentrate on this: My techniques, while criminally insane, cut through a massive amount of bureaucratic red tape.

Your country is devolving from its original pretense of democracy into something as wild and new and unspoiled as the golden frontiers from which this myth sprang. The United States of America is now on the verge of becoming the launchpad for a radical and unfettered new system: the Holy American-Pluto-Monopogarchy, an über-imperial, wild-style, free-market, XX-treme-o Theo-Capitalissimus Maximus . . . juiced on 'roids. A Thuggo-Ecclesiastical, Oligo-Pentagonarchy-al-Olio. With an attitude. It's indescribable. Anyway, to quote *Beyond the Valley of the Dolls*: "It's my happening, and it's freaking me out!"

Just trust me: You will obey. You *want* to obey. You will *love* obeying. Microserfs with proper unquestioning loyalty and abject servitude will achieve total buy-in.

Imperial tyranny, as history will support and any taste-making trend-spotter will tell you, is the wave of our future. And I am just the Sociopath of Divine Birth to drive it all home.

Come, my American children, into my soothing embrace of malls and multiplexes. Let the loving but stern Father of your Fatherland extend you the credit to buy the valuable prizes you deserve.

You're worth it!

In short, relax. Everything is under control, exactly as it has been in one way or another since the dawn of recordable history. You really have no idea how under control everything is.

A NOTE ON TRANSLATION FROM THE COAUTHOR

I was just following orders.
—Cintra Wilson

1

HELLO, I'M RULING CLASS, AND YOU'RE NOT: LESSONS MY IMPERIAL DYNASTY TAUGHT ME

Money to get power, power to protect money.
—Tacky motto of the otherwise
fabulous Medici family

The privileged man, whether he be privileged
politically or economically, is a man
depraved in intellect and heart.
—Mikhail Bakunin, anarcho-syndicalist

My darling Americans, what I am about to tell you may shake your very core beliefs and values as citizens of the United States. You may feel outraged, furious and even violent. You may think, How *dare* you, Caligula, you ancient cross-dressing greaseball. We should crucify you up against the nearest chain-link immigration fence.

But, lo: Though the universal truths I am about to radiate upon you may burn your mind, this pain will seem a small price to pay for the throbbing enlightenment that follows. A sociopolitical tequila baptism, as it were.

Incredibly, a vast number of fine, earnest Americans still believe that America isn't governed by a tiny, rotating, closed circuit of hereditary monarchies. Believers will cite various historical exceptions to this rule until the veins stand out in their necks. But they're missing the point.

Americans rightfully cherish their narrative of America as a class-free society, with no caste system that designates certain persons to be elevated to the status of royalty, and others to be unclean, leprous filth from inferior bloodlines, deserving of inhumane punishments for their willingness to consort with demons, who weaken the fabric of society as a whole and directly undermine your personal quality of life.

These convictions, while laudable, are totally off.

Sky God–fearing Americans believe that no matter what trailer park they were born under, if they work hard and earn university degrees and piles of professional laurels on a ceaseless upward trajectory toward fine goals, and eat their vegetables and love Mom and Old Glory with enough diligence and zeal, the American system guarantees that their presence will be welcome in any dining room on Earth.

In extremely rare and exceptional examples, I concede, this is occasionally true.

If, for example, you happen to be a wonderful man-insect—an electrical engineer with the tirelessly industrious and unemotional mind of a large bee, like

Bill Gates, who in savantlike fashion was able to create an entire technological hive culture and a personal net worth that at one point was roughly equal to the combined value of the entire bottom 40 percent of the Great Unlaundered American population—then, yes.

The secret envoys of the Divine Class, in such rare cases, may drive up in a sleek black armored car, tap you on the shoulder, hand you a powdered wig and invite you to game of croquet in the Bosquet de l'Etoile of our fabulous Versailles in space.

But this is unlikely. Allow me to share an intimate secret: *It's a pretty exclusive little clique.* We don't really want or need new friends.

It is important to remember that Man, like the baboon and other species woven into the tapestry of our colorful genetic ancestry, is a political animal who has always sought to dominate his fellow animals by as vast and terrifying a margin as possible.

Only an excruciatingly select and virtually invisible demographic sliver of you will ever achieve the Neverland Voodoo Ranch mind-set required of true leadership: unbounded and absolute self-regard, combined with a supremely ambivalent moral nonchalance and a desire to consume, in bonfire-like fashion, everything and everyone worth consuming. It is a parallel world: a wish-world-become-real, created and reinforced each day by the collective self-serving rationalizations and ideological, guilt-evading groupthink of other unnaturally, superbly rich people.

These are the truly blessed—the ideological diamond-eaters!—who, with tunnel-vision egomania, a totally amoral Will to Supreme Power, and zero-sum, winner-take-all instincts, eventually make convenient, temporary alliances (albeit with vast mistrust and reluctance) for the sake of uniting their powers just enough to collaboratively gouge the lower, insignificant quadrants of the populace, thereby doubling and redoubling each other's colossal and obscene wealth. Each does this in the hope that in the end, they will finally be able to embugger and impoverish everyone else in their conspiracy and ascend to the grand prize: achieving greater wealth and influence than everyone else, thereby protecting the enduring might of their brands/dynasties and their ability to drink the blood of peasants as simply as if they had pop-up sport-nipples.

In short, you've had it awfully easy up until now. All the grown-ups have worked really hard, and tiptoed around while you were sleeping for a couple hundred years, to preserve your belief for as long as possible that there is no artistocracy, and all boys are heroes, and all girls are princesses, and you'll get money under your pillow for all your lost teeth, and you'll all grow up to sing on television. It's democratic T-ball! Everyone gets a trophy.

(Or do you just *think* you'll get a trophy someday? Haven't you been waiting an awfully long time for your trophy? How come that other kid already got a really *big* trophy?)

In thrall to the natural, inexorable, cyclic states of empire, the American government is finally beginning to sprout hair on its lip and smell like all the others, and is almost beginning to resemble an adult superpower, in regard to the vast, regrettable and boringly predictable evils of monarchic leadership.

The Chinese had this empire-degeneration mambo wired. They actually devised a formula for it, since after several centuries a pattern emerged that was so regular you could pretty much set your sundial by it:

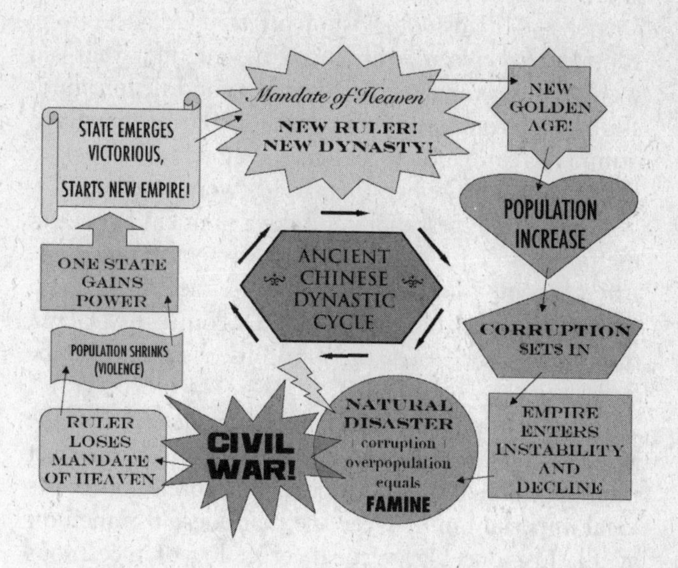

Repeat, ad nauseum, for thousands of years.

It's high time you Americans got the blonde highlights out of your eyes and noticed that virtually monarchic dynasties have been front and center in your civilian leadership since this country's infancy. The recent administration may have been more arrogant, artless and hubristic when it came sticking Dad's big black imperial glove up legal annals where it didn't belong, but some hereditary despots are more tactful than others, and some wear leather jodhpurs and a blood-diamond tiara and carry a stun baton.

It's so painfully obvious, but Americans still get upset when you say these things. You don't like to hear that your government is aging badly. America cherishes a delusional vision of itself as a carefree, sun-freckled tween, which is why your fifty-year-old women buy saline-enhanced breasts and denim miniskirts, and your men buy televisions large enough to mimic the comparative size they seemed to be back in their childhoods, when their heads were smaller.

I humbly suggest that you take a moment to gaze at the family tree of a few members of your ruling class. Any of them. Take your pick. The Kennedys, the Lees, the Bushes, the Rockefellers, the DuPonts, the Daleys, the Dulleses, the Gores, the Johnsons, the Adamses, the Roosevelts . . .

Actually, don't bother. I always suspected that the Washington Monument wasn't modeled on an erect phallus so much as on a modern interpretation of the ideal imperial family tree: one that doesn't branch off at all. Just one big, vertical, erect log of incestuous monarchy (with all the power in the world concentrated right on the end of my tip, ho ho).

It's an odds-on favorite that if one laid enough Mormon genealogy charts end to end, one could prove either that all these fine families are related or that at least they've all laid each other end to end. Political alliances, after all, have always been made by marriage (Marcus Vipsanius Agrippa and Julia the Elder? Meet Arnold Schwarzenegger and Maria Shriver, blah blah blah, and nineteen centuries of examples in between). The Gores are related to the Kennedys are related to the Carters and now the Shriverneggers. I have it on good authority that a relative of either the Bush or the Gore families has had a candidate in every presidential election for the last 190 years . . . and both families happen to be distantly related to the queen of England (which just goes to show you that even while debutantes may have jumped ship and married poets and gurus in the sixties, these ideological and eugenic detours corrected rather quickly once the girls figured out that communal goat farming wasn't as fun as getting their legs waxed and lunching at the Hay-Adams).

America's drunkest president, the confederate Franklin Pierce, "The Hero of Many a Well-Fought Bottle" (1853–1857), in typical ruling-class family tradition, got off scot-free for running down a woman while drunk-driving a horse. Pierce happens to be the great-great-great-great-uncle of George W. Bush, another outstanding alcoholic president, who, in the tradition of ancestor Pierce, is also a contender for the title of Worst President in U.S. History (which just goes to show you that the applejack doesn't fall too far from the tree, and the jug usually hits other people).

American dynasties are modeled, however lamely and furtively, on European dynasties—the Carolingians, the Hapsburgs, the Stuarts, the Romanovs, the Hohenzollerns, the Captetians, the Schleswig-Holstein-Sonderburg-Glücksburgs, et al. (who, no doubt, modeled themselves after the infinitely superior Julio-Claudians). These namby blue-blooded simps dominated European history with extreme prejudice and *openly* and *aggressively* pursued the agenda of securing the longevity of their dynasties (mostly by pursuing the delicate art of producing heirs cowardly enough not to kill their parents but robust enough to take over their leadership after allowing said parents to expire in a nonpatricidal fashion).

It's just heartbreakingly *silly* to imagine the American version of leadership isn't following exactly the same game plan; they've certainly tried to emulate European royalty in everything *else* (except, perhaps, for acknowledging honest and credible assessments of what, exactly, they're doing in positions of leadership).

It's as true now as it was in the year 39: Those of you not born to powerful families, I am afraid, are a virtually invisible bacteria—submicroscopic pistons in the vast collective engine of national entropy, working facelessly toward the greater purpose of rotting the body of an empire that has already begun to seep gray ooze.

And it's all your fault ☺.

But there is hope. Hope. Yes, and change. Change, and hope.

Me!

All right, yes, I hear you saying that if covert hereditary monarchy is America's problem, I am not an obvious cure.

You could say that I had greatness thrust upon me. As a blue-blood-engorged member of the divine Julio-Claudian dynasty, I perhaps did inherit sharper shoes for the horse fight.

But believe me, it's no cakewalk, being "to the palace born."

Ruling-class families are, in virtually every case, *wildly fucked-up.*

It's an occupational hazard. Everyone is a chief, nobody is an Indian. *I-love-you-I-kill-you.* As we all learned from the great god Cronos, sometimes eating your children is your only hope for a long reign.

In addition to being haplessly crippled by generations of incest, we are also prone to hemophilia, epilepsy, feeblemindedness, extremely distracting perversions, substance addiction, male-pattern baldness, poor impulse control, megalomania, sadism and a vast, almost psychotic loathing and total mistrust of all other family members and all human beings in general.

In the interest of transparency, I must disclose to you that in the follies of my youth, I myself experimented with hallucinatory substances such as mandragora, hemlock, aconite, henbane, belladonna and assorted mushrooms. I blame the pressures, demands and abuses I suffered in my childhood as a son of the beloved war hero Germanicus, a really cold, aloof tight-ass who often thrashed me for normal childhood play, such as setting small oil fires or putting my thumbs in my sisters.

I was only five years old, back in the year 17, when Germanicus was granted an official triumph by the senate.

White bulls were sacrificed. All of Rome came out to line the roads to greet the procession—mainly, I think, to watch the captive German barbarians get paraded through the streets on their way to being eaten alive by wild dogs.

In a brilliant bit of PR spin, my brothers, sisters,

mother and I were all allowed to ride with my father in his chariot for this honor.

The commoners thought we were just adorable: the perfect Roman family.

Think of it this way: We were young John F. Kennedy in a black Lincoln town car convertible with Jackie, Bobby, John-John and Caroline—only we were all a lot better-looking, and Jack had just won the NASCAR Sprint Cup Championship.

This was the first day it really hit me that my family was vastly different than everyone else's. We were us, and everyone else clearly wasn't. This obviously meant something.

My father refused to let me stand in front of him in the chariot, even though I was much smaller, and the crowd obviously derived great enjoyment from seeing my bright impish face, my tousled blond curls, and the miniature combat uniform my mother had me wear.

I was finally allowed a little place to perch off to the side, and that is when I saw them.

The Roman people.

The lumpy-faced, stench-breathing, black-toothed, subliterate, fish-head- and goat-dung-smelling, burlap-sheet-wearing Roman citizenry.

They were just enthralled, shouting our names and adoring us as we passed.

I knew my destiny.

I knew that someday all the misdirected love of these chinless human sock-puppets would be mine, and mine alone.

I understood their roles and mine in an instant. All

those pathetic, filthy, mindless sewer-class mud-persons of Rome were destined to become my private erector set.

As individuals, they were as worthless as bolts. But organized and manipulated in bulk, they had the same potential as . . . big *sacks* of bolts. Collectively, they were a really big blunt object that I would be able to hit other nations with.

This is exactly what I went on to do.

It would be this way because it had always been this way: Somebody from my family would always move into the palace, to direct and channel the barely conscious energies of the otherwise inconsequential lives of the average citizenry, and to point their pitifully dim and tiny lives toward a glorious *purpose*.

And that glorious purpose is ME.

It was later suggested by such big girl's blouses as the wino historian Tacitus that I, a mere child, had taken part in the conspiracy to cause my father's death.

This is only because I had a rather cuddly friendship with Martina, his poisoner, who taught me how to arrange infant Negro corpses and petrified cats around the house in a way that my father found metaphysically spooky. Please. Nowadays, it would barely pass for Halloween decor.

I suppose all boys feel an innate guilt over the death of their father. Fortunately, I am not all boys. Germanicus gave a great media face, but in truth, I found the old man to be a bit of a cunt, and I was more than happy to help a loose coalition of mutually interested parties frighten him off to the Underworld.

I don't think he ever liked me very much, either.

I inherited everything the hard way. *Nepotism* is from the Latin word *nepos*, meaning "nephew" or "grandson," which, in my family, meant "poisoned," "decapitated," or occasionally, "exiled forever to a tiny fucking rock in the middle of the ocean, close to what we presumed was the sucking, clifflike drop at the edge of the world."

I did what I had to do. It wasn't totally beyond the realm of possibility that he might have come for me first. Imperial children are necessary, but they're not exactly *wanted*.

In the Ottoman Empire, after 1607, sultans' children were routinely murdered at birth, lest they should forget who's boss. King Yongjo of Korea locked his son, Sado, into a wooden chest and left him there until he cacked (although few persons have ever been named more aptly than Sado, a seriously twisted urnful of nasty with a thing for killing maids. That's a *very* expensive weekend at the Chateau Marmont . . .). Oh, and if your father, like most tyrants, has a paranoid streak? You may as well save him the trouble and just hurl yourself down the Gemonian stairs on Father's Day.

Nadir Shah of Persia suspected his son Reza Qoli Mirza was plotting something nefarious, so he went ahead and had him *blinded*. Czar Peter the Great tortured his son Alexis to death, trying to get him to confess to some scheme. Ivan the Terrible bashed in his son's forehead with a spear. It is suspected that King Erik IV of Sweden beat his daughter Cecile to death for no good reason whatsoever. Stalin's son was captured as a German prisoner of war, but Stalin turned down an offer to swap him out for a German soldier.

Thanks, Imperial Dad.

Like I said, you do NOT want to be a member of the ruling class.

Your greatest hope is to know your place in society and desist in your painful, galling delusion of upward mobility.

Let me tell you why.

Americans, since they have been deprived of the presence of divine royalty (and because they have absolutely no idea how fucked-up it is), *crave being oppressed by it even more than they loathe and envy it.* I believe that's how America ended up with such a virulent strain of celebrity.

You *loo-o-o-o-o-ve* your ruling class. You rightfully perceive yourselves as snubbed by the real .00000000001 percent of the population, yet you worship your oppressors and aspire to be their pals and fans and confidants in a Stockholm syndrome–like fashion. This social phenomenon echoes throughout history and junior high school.

You love us so much that you even imitate the awful things we do. Lesser French noblemen, seeing their betters pissing on the outside wall of Versailles, would promptly ride home and piss on the walls of their own manors, just to give them that "Versailles smell."

It's cute. You're like little girls trying to walk around in your evil stepmommy's latex stiletto hip-waders and PVC dominatrix harness.

You lumpenproletariat don't really want to overthrow your monarchs and dictators. What you *really* want is to "get the look for less."

(And you have to admit, pissing on walls is *fun*.)

Anyway, my point is this: Those of you born to less powerful families than mine really don't have any idea how to use the tools of unlimited nepotistic power, irredeemable corruption, unlimited resources and the unchecked aggression to wield them all to the fullest possible extent. You haven't been bred for it, and you should thank your lucky stars you weren't.

Power corrupts, but absolute power is brain-fryingly hallucinogenic.

It's like any hard drug—unless you grew up doing it, you're a lightweight. With great power comes great responsibility; but with absolute power, your mind becomes clamped with intolerable pressure from every possible angle, until it finally spits itself inside out like a six-dimensional eyeball made of white fire. At that point, "absolute responsibility" reveals itself as the Zen paradox of *absolutely no responsibility or accountability whatsoever*.

I told you. You just weren't raised to understand these things. If you don't have a built-in immunity to the toxicities of leadership, you'd never have the stomach for it. Sure, you'd have fun indulging a bit of bureaucratic kleptomania and zipping wounded raccoons into a leather duvet cover with your dissidents for a little while, but at the end of the day, if you don't have the in-house training to oppress with the big dogs, you'd probably just end up like all the other grubby little tyrants who didn't have the proper pedigree, trying to look dignified in a dirty little room while your head gets pulled off by angry guys in ski masks.

Just trust me. I know how to do this. For peons of low birth like yourselves, unbridled domination of your vast American empire with your rude will is an ungraspable concept. But I am born to this task. America and I were made for each other.

You are going to need me, because on the subject of nepotism and dynasty, I must issue a dire warning.

I prophesy that young George Prescott Bush III could present a direct threat to my divine authority in 2016.

Jeb Bush should have eaten George Prescott while he was still small enough to swallow whole. This boy is very handsome; he has thick black hair and speaks Spanish. He looks like Enrique Iglesias in a Turnbull & Asser suit. It is my opinion that he will be groomed to emotionally manipulate stadium crowds of fearful, lower-class young Jesus-lovers into a weeping, Elvis-worthy sexual panic, in concert with an organized, psychological operation of relentless global PR carpet bombing of a price and magnitude ordinarily associated with Exxon. The full weight of the Bush legacy's war chest will finally buy the love and total complicity of the cool youth vote: early-adopters, the extreme-sports community, and/or whatever the godforsaken future of Facebook- and MySpace-style social networking holds. A brave new frontier of image-making will mold young George Prescott into one part Che Guevara, one part young Ronald Reagan, and six parts Napoléon.

Combined with his family's patented banana-republic-style tilting of electronic voting machines, George Prescott will be unstoppable.

So, here's a little trick I picked up over the centuries: Take pains to ensure that he becomes addicted to hookers, OxyContin or anonymous gay sex in public men's rooms.

I believe this is the duty of all Americans who do not wish to hand over their children at birth to be trained as bullet-polishers for Halliburton.

Go get him, all you hot, hot, American whores, drug fiends and daring young homosexual men. Go get George Prescott.

(I shall dispatch the political ambitions of Chelsea Clinton and the Gore sisters myself, by taking them as imperial concubines. Keep your enemies closer, as they say. Give me a month, and I'll have them all wearing Bulgari belly-chains and matching white stretch-lace tap pants, lounging around on muscle relaxants at the Oval Office, ovulating together.)

You see? This won't be so hard.

I will be the brains; you will be the brawn. Together we will make America the greatest totalitarian military dictatorship in the history of mankind.

Tyranny is about to become your new best friend.

2

HOW TO WIN FRIENDS AND INFLUENCE HISTORY; OR, HOW I LEARNED TO STOP WORRYING AND LOVE DOMESTIC PROPAGANDA

Whoever controls the media, the images,
controls the culture.
—Allen Ginsberg

By the skilful and sustained use of propaganda, one
can make a people see even heaven as hell or an
extremely wretched life as paradise.
—Adolf Hitler

Honestly, I think we should just trust our president
in every decision that he makes and we should
just support that.
—Britney Spears, on the invasion of Iraq

In a way, your grandma was right—TV *did* finally destroy your mind.

Joseph Goebbels, the Nazi minister of propaganda, once said, "When I hear the word 'culture,' I reach for my revolver." Goebbels was half right, but being a deeply square and fussy little Nazi, he naturally failed to make the bigger point: Culture *is* the revolver.

Ah, Deutschland really would have been über alles if the Nazis had only had television and the type of PR techniques we have now, after fifty years of psychiatrists working for ad agencies on Madison Avenue. Poor Goebbels is really percolating in *der inferno* now, thinking about the all-pervasive media empire that would be suckling from his teat of menace if he'd only been born in the fifties.

Perception is reality. Media is omnipresent. Therefore, he who controls the media controls perception, and therefore controls reality TV, and therefore controls reality.

Take, for example, the ongoing triumphs of Rupert Murdoch—the Alexander of international media, who, after finally conquering the *Wall Street Journal*, now owns a powerful 62 percent controlling interest in the thoughts, information, taste and opinions of all human beings, unto the point of papal infallibility.

When Murdoch brazenly thumped his rock-hard septuagenarian johnson on the table at the 2007 World Economic Forum in Davos and admitted that his Fox News channel pulled a classic wag-the-dog-style, domestic propaganda consent-manufacturing in the drum-beating up to the war in Iraq, it was gorgeous. A really blithe acknowledgment of a supreme mass brainwashing that essentially said, "Yes, as a matter of fact, I am the Word and the Light. There's nothing you or anyone else can do about it. Suck me gently, planet Earth."

The result of this bombshell, answer-to-every-conspiracy-theorist's-dreams admission: Yawn.

Were cop cars overturned in the streets? Was the Sydney waterfront seized by a militia of armed aborigines? Did Americans commit mass suicide in a wave of national self-loathing?

No.

Q: Why?

A: Larry Birkhead. Genetic father of Anna Nicole Smith's hapless orphan infant. Way more interesting. Much bigger story.

Or so they say. But then again, "they" are usually Rupert Murdoch.

It's *perfection.*

Most hilariously of all, "the media" are blamed for this failure of intellectual values—cowardly journalists in particular. This is sort of like criticizing a chain gang that has been thrown into a shark tank for not performing better water ballet.

(Such is the irrational bliss of tyranny! ☺)

Nowadays, fame and politics have split into distinct and separate bicameral parts, but in my day, the emperor was not just the political and religious center of the world, but charismatic dictators and rock stars were virtually the *same thing*. Serious Roman politicians cultivated auras of pop celebrity much more brazenly than politicians today.

The cult of charismatic personality is a vital weapon

in the political arsenal; it's the easiest way to touch, thrill and influence the biggest, dumbest amount of people, all at the same time.

Nero, for example, fancied himself a singer and actor on par with David Hasselhoff—only he was execrable at both, and also one of the most profligate motherfuckers in history.

In my administration, I pledge a return to the glory days of old-fashioned absolute dictatorship: Politics and pop culture are going to merge back into one big ugly Frankenstein baby.

American presidents have known they have to get the pop thing figured out, but they haven't quite nailed it yet. They've flirted with it, lamely, but have yet to really roll out a balls-to-the-wall, glitz-spangled Liza Minelli special. Americans are now too overstimulated and spoiled by choices to be properly manipulated by the old rallies that used to boil nationalistic fervor—billowing flags, unctuous marching band music, and a white man in a dark suit speaking in comforting Judeo-Christian jingoisms.

Politicians, thus far, generally blow it pretty badly when they try to embrace hipness. Remember Richard Nixon, trying in his ashen, bulbous honky way to seize the love of the youth with his fist-pumping "Sock it to me!" clunker? Bill Clinton tried to harness the panty-throwing vote by wearing Ray-Bans and playing the saxophone, then having Leonardo DiCaprio interview him on the state of the environment. The Bush administration had Britney Spears appear on TV to express her support for the invasion of Iraq and beseech her legions of young fans to "trust" the commander in chief. The best thing George W. Bush probably ever did for his popularity was dress up in a leather bomber jacket like Tom Cruise from *Top Gun*. Bush II learned how to work this drag act from Ronald Reagan, who made himself an icon by butching up in a rootin' tootin' John Wayne, fantasy cowboy costume. Lasso the semiotics of American machismo and you've got yourself a leading brand!

(Unfortunately, Bush failed to achieve semiotic presidential superpowers with his "Mission Accomplished" flight-suit codpiece, which, I think we can all agree, was going a little too far—like, "Cher at the Oscars" too far. Bob Mackie at least would have insisted that the president emerge from the plane in a sudden eruption of red, white and blue ostrich feathers and a Swarovski crystal gas mask.

Still, it was a logical, if failed, effort. I predict that history won't regard George W. Bush's biggest mistake as his war on Iraq, but his refusal to show more chest hair.)

Winning the attention of Americans is like hypnotizing chickens. You must fascinate the prehistoric reptile mind: the tiny, primitive limbic system, repository of intangible, irrational, emotional impulses that drive a human being to buy a particular car or a particular candidate, and to prefer sleeping on an actual mattress as opposed to wet gravel.

In an era of information-saturation, future Americans will need their president to be shinier and more distracting, with pyrotechnics and Elton John glasses.

L.A. circles the drain of Fame while Washington circles the drain of Power while Wall Street circles the drain of Money, but the biggest players in all three locales are the morbid narcissists, because you just can't tear your eyes off them.

Not for nothing is the checklist of symptoms for a tyrant, a superstar, a successful corporation and a psychopath exactly the same: an exaggerated sense of self-importance; flagrant hubris; a prolonged, if not eternal, adolescence; an amplified sense of personal entitlement; abusive behavior toward inferiors (everyone not them); unchecked extravagance; exhibitionism; shoplifting; excessive cosmetic surgery; casual torture; total lack of empathy; unhealthy relationships with people, pets and motor vehicle . . . the list goes on.

What really separates ordinary citizens from emperors, monsters, superstars and immortal leading brands?

"Normal" people simply don't have the *huevos* to withstand disgrace. They usually don't use fire-hose blasts of negative attention as an opportunity to run out and court more negative attention, by throwing up on the prime minister, or purposefully running down the parking valet, or instigating an "ethnic cleansing" or "accidentally" shaving their crotch in a public water fountain.

But, as Uncle Rupert has shown us, disgrace is crucial for driving the public's attention where you want it. The point is to enable the president to control *more* attention by *harnessing the power of disgrace himself.*

He really needs to *own* it, punk-rock style, in order to funnel your gaze into exactly the dirty little sweet hole where he wants it.

This is bold-thought leadership in action, and it requires *talent*.

We have some incredible disgrace-artists working in the business today who are really pointing the way to our political future.

Take Lindsay Lohan, former Disney child star turned whipping-chippy of the yellow press. She's up! She's down. She's clean! She's writhing around with no pants in a hotel lobby. She's pole dancing with her mom. She's practically a Judith Regan edition of the Book of Job.

Lindsay's personal issues considerably helped to eclipse the dismissal of the U.S. attorneys controversy.

Her second arrest for DUI-cum-cocaine-possession, on July 24, 2007, was enormously helpful in distracting the news cycle away from the fact that on July 25, 2007, the U.S. House Judiciary Committee tried to crack down on White House counsel Harriet Miers and Chief of Staff Joshua Bolten for ignoring their subpoenas regarding the probe into the dismissal of the U.S. attorneys.

Lohan was sentenced to a day in jail and ten days' community service on August 23, 2007; Attorney General Alberto Gonzales announced his resignation on August 27, 2007. Who, pray tell, got more coverage?

Did Betsy Ross do more for her country than Lindsay?

Paris Hilton is, in fact, a Warholian genius of media manipulation. If Marilyn Monroe and Princess Diana were "candles in the wind," and Anna Nicole Smith was a bonfire in a hailstorm, and Lindsay Lohan is an electric toaster oven thrown intentionally into a

Jacuzzi, then Paris Hilton is a strobe light in an epilepsy ward.

If you don't regard Paris Hilton with the proper awe and trembling, consider this: Paris reportedly charges $200,000 to show up at a party for twenty minutes. Just to give this price tag some sense of proportion, the average per capita annual income in Iraq in 2004 was $422.

It would take the average Iraqi over twenty years to earn one minute with Paris Hilton, or around twenty-four Iraqis one year to divide and share that one minute with Paris between them. (This would be a complete waste of money unless they could use that one minute to swallow her jewelry, handbag and shoes.)

Paris managed to turn a prison sentence into a mainstream career move—a grand Kabuki production as titillating and meaningless as when she kisses her own sister (unlike, for example, when I make out with *my* sister).

If I were Paris, I might have used this twenty-three-day opportunity in the clink to become a Black Muslim and great spiritual leader, and write *Mein Kampf II: Bigger Bones for Blondie*. I would also have had a scorching lesbian affair with a fellow inmate, which would have been "secretly captured" on a guard's cell phone (*The Banlieue Is Burning: One Night Just Outside Paris*).

She did, however, manage to begin her jail sentence on June 5, 2007, the very same day that I. Lewis "Scooter" Libby Jr., the former chief of staff to Vice President Dick Cheney, was sentenced to thirty months in prison after being convicted of perjury and obstruction of justice in the grand jury investigation of the leaking of CIA operative Valerie Plame's identity.

Was this sheer luck? Pure coincidence?

Or was it *raw patriotism*?

Consider Britney Spears, Our Lady of Perpetual Humiliation.

The "Britney Industrial Complex," according to an article in *Condé Nast Portfolio*, brings in 20 percent of the U.S. paparazzi business; Spears cover shots spike tabloid sales 33 percent for an estimated value of between $110 million and $120 million annually, of which Britney reportedly earns less than 10 percent—which is still quite a good living when you consider that it primarily consists of being dragged in and out of courtrooms and hospitals while crying and strapped to a gurney. Britney, in effect, took over Michael Jackson's job.

On February 7, 2007, Britney Spears left rehab and made global headlines by shaving her head.

On February 8, 2007, reality TV catastrophe Anna Nicole Smith made international news by being found dead in a Florida hotel room.

On February 9, 2007, a jaw-dropping report by the U.S. Defense Department's inspector general was released into the media bloodstream, stating that the Pentagon "purposely manipulated" intelligence in the months leading up to the invasion of Iraq.

. . . but we were still talking about Britney and Anna Nicole, so the report didn't make quite the splash it might have, in, say, the seventies, before these things were properly coordinated. But the good news is, we all got to be as surprised by this information as if it were brand new when ex–White House press secratary Scott McClellan's tell-all book came out fifteen months later!

On November 29, 2006, Britney Spears, out partying with Paris Hilton, was photographed exiting a car without any panties on. On December 6, while we were still reeling from this shock and awe and trying to analyze what it meant, the Iraq Study Group Report was released, calling the situation in Iraq "grave and deteriorating" and calling for a change in strategy, including the removal of most of our troops.

Then, just to really cake on the confusion, on December 7, seven U.S. attorneys were dismissed by the Department of Justice.

Who can keep track of such informational miasmata?

But one truth remains certain. As a caption on TMZ.com read, "Britney loses it, the world watches." This was a rare and pungent truth from a news outlet that is more or less the journalistic equivalent of unprotected sex with diseased baboons.

Britney's real occupation, of course, has been to suck enough real critical and substantive news out of the air to be the Typhoid Mary of information mangling. And I believe this is the way of the future. This is exactly what an American president *needs to do*.

There is no good press and bad press. Fame is made of quantities of attention, not qualities, and is therefore binary: There is Press or No Press. Not Hot and Cold, but Hot and Off. Attention is the currency in a world with too many people—whoever arrests the news cycle long enough to make themselves the topic, wins.

Personal disgrace and humiliation will always dominate the news cycle exponentially more than skeevy policy maneuvers of questionable legality. Even at top levels, such shenanigans require a trained priest-class of lawyers to decode. (You're not supposed to understand these documents; they are built to ensure maximum, eye-bleeding levels of boredom, inscrutability and obscurantism. You, average citizen, are excluded from needing to speak Law for your own *pleasure and convenience.*)

But here's a little lesson in gobbledygook, just for yucks: The word *tragedy* comes from the Greek *tragōidia*, which is a combination of the Greek words *tragos*, meaning "goat" (which is related to the word *gnaw*) and *odia,* meaning "song." It was basically an ancient Greek entertainment-industry term—*tragōidia*—meaning "goat-men sacrifice song." In any case, it definitely sheds some light on today's definition of "tragedy," which is "human sacrifice of a designated celebrity scapegoat (in order to distract attention from a glaring act of administrative elbow-fuckery)."

Fashions come and go, but humanity is always down for watching Christians (or their epoch-specific equivalent) get mauled by carnivores as stadium entertainment. The point and purpose of being a celebrity now is to become personae non panty, and perform rolling overdoses, public tantrums, galloping bulimia, suicide bids, binge divorces, barking fits of xenophobia, addictions to fentanyl, and lockdowns in correctional and rehabilitation institutions.

In short, celebrities' societal role is to live pitiably empty and ignorant lives with zero privacy while being chain-whipped by the flying monkeys of Rupert Murdoch (or his epoch-specific equivalent) during embarrassing political scandals, mass mind-control experiments, the mass extermination of the underprivileged, or other leadership crises in government.

This is not a new practice. This pagan ritual is as old as rocks.

Tag!

A goat is designated to embody "It"—"It" representing all the various sins, crimes, nightmares and diseases of the community—and everyone chases the terrible goat off the cliff and the national psyche is thereby healed from the crimes and issues that everyone is too powerless and ignorant to understand. Hosanna!

I've already got some great ideas for the scapegoating of certain celebrities that do not meet with my approval.

As punishment for cycling with members of the last administration, Lance Armstrong will be forced to wear a very tight stack of yellow rubber bracelets around his only remaining testicle for several months. For charity, of course.

Tucker Carlson may still be useful as an all-purpose, party-line-mewling lap-Nazi, but he is really just a sneevy, mawkish, oversoft priggot whose very being repulses me personally. Since Tucker Carlson's head and bouffant is so huge, and his skull is so dense as to be barely supported by the neck of his toneless, oversize, spongy marshmallow-chick body, he shall be rented out as entertainment for children's birthday parties. Small children should be allowed to hit Tucker

Carlson's head with sticks like a piñata. They will, no doubt, find it to be full of a kind of whipped snot-praline nougat fondant.

Finally, I shall throw him (along with fellow Anglo-frips Willie Geist and Bill Hemmer) into a little boutique prison camp I keep in Ashgabat, where they will go through a procedure I like to call "Wipe That Smug Face Off Your Smile."

Then, for my birthday-party entertainment, I vow to have my guard aggressively twist Carlson's bow tie around and around like a propeller until his head falls off.

Some of these punishments may be actually useful.

Since it is extremely difficult to find women who are as universally disliked as Ann Coulter, I believe she should be placed on different borders to incite incidents of violence that eventually lead to shooting wars. I may drop her off on the border of Iran in a little black dress with a copy of *The Satanic Verses* and let her mouth do the rest.

Nero set fire to Rome in 64 and he needed a real media-magnet of a scapegoat, so he started persecuting Christians.

"[Christians] were covered with wild beast skins and torn to death by dogs, or were fastened to crosses and burned to serve as lamps by night," said Tacitus.

And the best part was, they were completely innocent!

In the slave era, America had witches and whipping boys; now you have drug-sucking, sexually promiscuous young starlets who get hounded to death by paparazzi in order to heal national shames of an inscrutably complex and confusing nature.

You call it bread and circuses; I call it . . . showtime!

You want to rid yourself of national malaise? Focus your limited attention units on Hollywood's kooky death-trip blondes and exciting serial psycho killers. Who has time to understand the labyrinthine roads through congressional bribery, policy fixing, or military Keynesianism?

But you *do* understand, and get to be hardy participants in, the prevailing cultural trope I whimsically like to call "Death to the Slut."

Admit it. America is really not so different from Somalia: You love to stone the adulteress just as much as anyone under sharia law. You just prefer to psychologically torture your fallen women to death because it takes longer. I *understand.*

We punish our societal whipping blondes because we *understand their crimes.* Believe me, spanking naughty starlets is much healthier for the nation than trying to de-garble the rhetoric of Washington lawyers.

The yellow press will hound a blonde into an early grave every five years or so, and parade her bloody bedsheets through the streets, and oily black gushers of inexhaustible tabloid revenue will blast up out of supermarket lines everywhere and fall upon us all like a dirty mist.

This is good for everyone.

You shouldn't feel *bad* when this happens. Your cultural framework guarantees a certain postmortem celebrity to persons who go out with a sufficient bang.

The Virginia Tech killer, for example, had this game wired. He played the media like a magic kazoo, taking a break between shootings to send the equivalent of a sociopathic MySpace page to NBC. It was a brilliantly prepared press package of video footage and self-styled *Taxi Driver*–style promo shots. He knew exactly how well it would work, because like so many other sociopaths-in-waiting, he was terribly impressed by America's obsessive interest in the Columbine High School killings.

The VA killer made the media complicit in his crime and helped inspire a nationwide rash of copycat shootings that week. Now, no legitimate psychopath need ever worry that his driving need for negative attention will go unmet—he just needs to make sure he kills a number of students greater than thirty.

In a way, school yard shootings are the American twin to Islamist suicide martyrs, who also celebrate themselves with the equivalent of jihadi YouTube videos. It is a tragic rock-stardom reserved as the last hope of the mute and invisible in a global climate where attention is the measure of success. Or, as George Bernard Shaw once said, "Martyrdom is the only way in which a man can become famous without ability."

(I say that martyrdom is a terrible waste, though, especially when Arab countries have so much *fabulous* singing talent out there just waiting to be exploited. You can hear Mariah Carey's melismatic influence on international singing styles during virtually every call to prayer. You say it's "hearts and minds" you want to win in the war against global jihadism? My first hundred days in office, I intend to air-drop digital video cameras, drum machines, and ceramic hairstyling flatirons, then stand back and watch the fans go wild for *Afghani Idol*! Don't fight the funk, just co-opt the opera. It's geopolitical *Cop Rock*.)

One last example: On August 17, 2006, U.S. District Judge Anna Diggs Taylor ordered that the National Security Agency's warrantless surveillance program be shut down, on the grounds of its being unconstitutional.

What was the bigger news item on August 17, 2006?

News from Thailand that a soft-fingered, doe-eyed, pastel-cardigan-wearing diaper-sniffer named John Mark Karr confessed to the murder of America's favorite dead, oversexed toddler: JonBenet Ramsey.

This didn't turn out to be actually *true*, but . . . never mind.

Which story do you remember happening?

You get my point.

When Gloria Arroyo ran for reelection in the Philippines in 2004, the *Economist* published an article titled "Democracy as Showbiz," and whinged that running for president in the Philippines is *so expensive* that celebrity name recognition has become crucial. Oh, horrors: Arroyo ran against a *movie star* and a *televangelist*.

America is *so* not the Philippines. Heck not.

Ronald Reagan: President.

Clint Eastwood: Mayor of Carmel.

Sonny Bono: Mayor of Palm Springs, member of the House of Representatives

Arnold Schwarzenegger: Kennedy.

Your future, if I am not elected? President of the United States Ben Affleck. You think I'm shitting you? Try wrapping your cake hole around the words "Secretary of Defense Matt Damon" a few times and feel the windchill factor.

The code is obvious—we know how to get your attention and keep it. The president could be winning your love and your Nielsen ratings anytime. The boys in the White House have just been too chickenshit to do it *right* so far because *overt* domestic propaganda still carries the taboo tang of the old Soviet Union. But—come on—what did we save Jessica Lynch for, anyway, if not to swing a well-placed chain saw through the American heartstrings and inject a little psychological Viagra into the national war-will?

Imagine this: a hot, sexy, hip, tanned president, with the photo-op love power of Camelot Jack Kennedy, plus Rachel Zoe styling. I am on TV every day, having a daily lunchtime chat with the nation. I have tousled, boyish, moussed hair, and I'm wearing a pink Indian-cotton shirt, open to expose just enough of my waxed chest. I sit cross-legged, having a picnic on the White House lawn, quadriceps bulging under my seersucker pants, no socks under my huaraches. Imagine my fabulously elegant First Lady, a striking mixed-race beauty (possibly Jessica Alba, after two years of total immersion in a foreign survivalist bootcamp) in couture vegetarian ballet flats, with loose black hair and castanets.

We dine casually, tossing clementine oranges across our Navaho picnic quilt to our friends Oprah, the Dalai Lama, Sir Richard Branson and Gwen Stefani.

Our lunch is a model for the new American diet: tomatoes from the White House organic victory garden, a light corn-and-millet salad. We discuss the most pressing issues of the day in terms of global human rights violations. Our domestic focus is primarily on ecological awareness and defending the poor from faceless corporate abuse. We meditate, discuss our bodies, our emotional well-being, the daily trials we face in our happy but oh-so-human marriage . . . and we discuss *you*, cherished American.

We care about you a *lot*, and want you to be *personally fulfilled*. That's why I, your beautiful, intelligent world leader, will remain compassionate, relaxed, hydrated, and on-camera for the better part of my term in office.

Then we'll give you something really zippy to look at, like our home bondage videos that the butler stole, or amateur footage of me urinating drunkenly on the side of the Jefferson Memorial, captured by a high school student on her cell phone.

I won't bore you to death with the usual humdrum, C-Span policy wonkmanship—I'll prove beyond a shadow of a doubt that Iranian president Mahmoud Ahmadinejad was directly responsible for not only 9/11, but also predatory mortgage practices, OxyContin and erectile dysfunction.

Dig this: Since I suffer from insomnia, I plan to also occasionally *serve as my own First Lady*. At night, I will wear women's bra-bikini sets and write the children's book *Jingo's First Christmas—by Jingo, the Arab-Hating White House Ocelot*.

Then, when you're really jittering and totally incapable of sustained concentration on anything important, I'll initiate the sport-killing of senior citizens and declare escort service hand jobs tax-deductible. That will keep you talking around the water cooler.

Remember: Not for nothing am I the guy who appointed a horse to the senate. Incitatus was a great horse and everything, but he wasn't elected to be the highest magistrate in Rome because he gave great *advice*, if you know what I mean.

I think we're beginning to understand each other, you and I.

3

THE REALITY CRISIS: MANAGING YOUR CONSENT AND MANUFACTURING YOUR PERCEPTIONS FOR PROFIT AND PROFIT

Francis Bacon pointed out long ago that "Knowledge itself is power." Secrecy gives those in government exclusive control over certain areas of knowledge, and thereby increases their power, making it more difficult for even a free press to check that power. In short, a free press is necessary for a democratic society to work effectively, but without access to information, its ability to perform its central role is eviscerated.

—Joseph Stiglitz

A popular Government, without popular information, or the means of acquiring it, is but a prologue to a farce or a tragedy; or, perhaps, both.

—James Madison

Naturally the common people don't want war . . .
Voice or no voice, the people can always be
brought to the bidding of the leaders. That is easy.
All you have to do is to tell them they are being
attacked, and denounce the pacifists for lack of
patriotism and exposing the country to danger. It
works the same in any country.

—Hermann Goering

Remember when crazy people used to walk up to you on the street with cardboard signs that said, HELP I AM BEING MURDERED, in big block letters, and if you made the mistake of giving them any eye contact, they'd start jabbering that the CIA did low-frequency electromagnetic experiments on their brain at Vacaville state prison that made them crazy?

Well, it's a safe bet those people were probably crazy even *before* the CIA got to them.

The war at home has always been waged between your ears. The battle to win your hearts and minds is still achieved by brainwashing, but nowadays, it's a fine art, and all very subtle. We no longer need Angela Lansbury to waddle around in a sandwich board covered with heavy Masonic symbolism, muttering unlikely word combinations like "tennis fruit."

In November of 2002, shortly before the 2003 invasion of Iraq, I enjoyed finding this headline in a quality tabloid by the name of the *National Examiner*:

EVIL SADDAM PAVES OVER
GARDEN OF EDEN.

The text in the article hit straight below the Bible Belt:

> Biblical scholars say the Garden of Eden bloomed where the Tigris and Euphrates rivers meet . . . Since the rise of the evil dictator [Hussein], the Garden looks more like the handiwork of Satan. Even the serpent that led to Adam and Eve's fall couldn't survive in the wasteland it's become. Vandals have killed the Tree of Life . . . And the battered wall guarding the area bears Saddam's message: "Down With America."

Now that, my friends, is *journalism*. Edward R. Murrow, if he had been alive, would have died instantly.

Anthropologist Tanya Luhrmann coined the term "interpretive drift"—which, loosely defined, is a slow drip, drip, drip, by which rational thinking can gradually become irrational. It's the way normal people become cult members, for example, or free Americans become slave labor for a totalitarian military dictatorship . . . A steady drip, drip, drip, that, after a while, results in a hole in your head big enough to hide a Buick or a genocide in.

Rupert Murdoch, owner of the ubiquitous holdings of News Corporation, is arguably the undisputed heavyweight Mother of All Drips, as it were, in terms of interpretive drift and our nation's slow, passive acceptance of nipple-flashing and cockeyed whoppers in lieu of objective "news"-type information.

Murdoch isn't alone in his mission.

Take, for example, the *Sunday Telegraph*, long considered the "house newspaper" of the U.K. Conservatives, which was until recently owned by the wholly disgraced Conrad Black.

(Drip.)

Or Reuters, which is owned by the Thomson Corporation, one of the world's largest information companies, with a multitude of corporate interests ranging from financial products to health care. Seventy percent of Thomson Corporation is still controlled by Canada's megarich, dynastic Thomson family.

(Drip.)

Time magazine had this heartstring-strangling headline in 2005:

DADDY, I WANT TO BE A MARTYR. CAN YOU GET ME AN EXPLOSIVE BELT?

This quote was from the nine-year-old son of Iraqi insurgent Abu Qaga al-Tamimi, a scary brown man who hates Freedom and whose whole job is to teach people how to strap bombs to themselves and give long, lingering hugs to U.S. Marines.

(I'm sure glad we're still at war with Iraq, because I'm terrified of nine-year-olds.)

Chris Matthews of MSNBC's *Hardball* once interviewed ex–General Electric chairman Jack Welch before a college audience in 2002:

UNIDENTIFIED MALE: What do you believe is the role of large businesses such as General Electric in this war on terrorism and in homeland security?

JACK WELCH: Well, I think we have to provide the goods and services that a government demands to have. I mean, if you look at the jet engines that are made today, they're made by General Electric.

Jack Welch, while CEO of General Electric, gave an enormous amount of money to the Republican Party over the years. GE has always been cozy with the GOP. Ronald Reagan was the spokesman for General Electric before he was president. Jeff Immelt replaced Jack Welch as GE's CEO, and he, too, gives boodles of money to the Republican Party.

General Electric, the world's second-largest company, had $1,011,657,364 worth of military-industrial contracts with your Department of Defense in 2007, according to militaryindustrialcomplex.com.

General Electric brings about eighty zillion "good things to life," including enormous finance and mortgage departments. It also just happens to own NBC, MSNBC, Universal, all the A&E Network (including the Biography Channel), Bravo, the SciFi Channel, the Sundance Channel, the USA Network, etc. And that's just in the States. It also owns Telemundo, which runs most TV South of the Border.

(DripDripDripDripDripDripDripDripDripDripDrip-DripDripDripDripDrip.)

Which brings us to the Rep. Henry A. Waxman

(D–Los Angeles) investigation of the 2000 presidential elections for the U.S. House Committee on Oversight and Government Reform.

To quote a Phil Rosenthal column from 2006 in the *Chicago Tribune*:

> There's [a] story—never fully proven, never fully refuted—alleging that Welch, while head of GE, which owns NBC, tried to intervene in NBC News' decision-making on election night of 2000, the too-close-to-call Al Gore-George Bush race.

Jack Welch was apparently hanging around the news desk at NBC's 30 Rockefeller Center that election night.

From an *L.A. Times* article by Megan Garvey:

> Waxman charged that eyewitness accounts of the evening "sharply conflict" with statements made by Welch and network officials that he had nothing to do with the premature decision to call the presidential election for Republican George W. Bush.

The article unpacks Waxman's allegations that there was hanky-panky in the newsroom that night. According to the *L.A. Times,* there were eyewitness accounts given to Waxman: "[Jack] Welch and other visitors 'distracted' NBC News Director of Elections Sheldon R. Gawiser with repeated questions about how his projection decisions were made."

Welch, according to Ms. Garvey's article, had

access to raw election data that weren't available to news anchors, writers, producers or other on-air reporters.

According to the story, after instruction about how to read this data, Welch concluded that Bush had won Florida and shared his analysis with Gawiser.

> Witnesses told Waxman that "at almost the same time, John Ellis—George W. Bush's cousin and Fox News' senior decision desk official—called both the Florida and the national election for George W. Bush. Immediately after this announcement, Mr. Welch was observed standing behind Dr. Gawiser with his hand on his shoulder, asking why NBC was not also calling the election for Bush."
>
> According to Waxman's sources, "shortly after this," Gawiser called the election for Bush. A similar call was made by all major television news outlets within minutes.

This apparently drove Waxman bonkers, because there were congressional hearings going on about the election reporting "snafus." Waxman asked the then–NBC News chief Andy Lack for internal video of the evening, which Lack said Waxman could have. Then later, Lack decided that wasn't a very good idea, and told Waxman he couldn't have the internal video.

Waxman was very bothered about this. He wrote that the incident raised "troubling questions." Waxman fired back at Lack with an eight-page letter, several months later, to NBC boss Bob Wright, "suggesting," according to the *L.A. Times*, that "Welch pressured news staffers to call Florida for Bush."

Waxman even threatened to seek a congressional subpoena for the internal video footage that NBC refused to give him. In 2006, Rosenthal spoke to Waxman's office to find out if the matter was ever resolved.

It wasn't—but maybe this is because Waxman's letter was made public on . . . get this . . .

. . . wait for it . . .

September 10, 2001.

(And then the next day was 9/11, 2001.)

By the time Waxman went public with his misgivings, it was a different world, and these niggling details about who said what, when, on election night, didn't seem very important to anyone anymore.

NBC officials did, however, make an internal decision to recommend isolating their election analysts and the decision desk, in order to protect them from "unnecessary interruptions" in the future.

Fortunately for America, General Electric happens to own the History Channel, as well as the Military History Channel, so the story will always be straight, from now on.

Because, as we all know, "He who controls history . . ."

Um . . . I forget the rest.

Anyway, none of this matters. Even if Jack Welch were indicted on anything so nebulous as the suction of influence his claw might have coerced out of Gawiser's shoulder, PR agencies like Burson-Marsteller can literally fix any reputation. You can go down to Bhopal and spray oven cleaner in the eyes of orphans for six months, just for fun, and they'll make it look like you were trying to correct their astigmatism.

PR is a multi-bazillion-dollar industry. There are far fewer journalists now than there are spin doctors. From the beginning of 2003 until the middle of 2005, the American government paid $1.6 billon to PR agencies and journalists—and behold! Everyone kept very snugly on-message.

James Bamford wrote, in his award-winning 2005 *Rolling Stone* article, "The Man Who Sold the War":

> One of the most powerful people in Washington, [John] Rendon is a leader in the strategic field known as "perception management," manipulating information—and, by extension, the news media—to achieve the desired result. His firm, the Rendon Group, has made millions off government contracts since 1991, when it was hired by the CIA to help "create the conditions for the removal of Hussein from power."

Depending on whom you talk to in the nebulous world of spooks, approximately half of what used to be considered CIA-type work—human-intelligence gathering, otherwise known as HUMINT (otherwise known as "spying on people")—is now frequently performed by private contractors like the Rendon Group, "corporate spooks," who (just like Rent-a-Dirty-Little-War outfits like DynCorp, Blackwater,

KBR, and Triple Canopy) also offer the great advantage and convenience of being completely unaccountable to Congress.

From Bamford's article:

> Another newly formed propaganda operation in which Rendon played a major part was the Office of Global Communications, which operated out of the White House and was charged with spreading the administration's message on the War in Iraq . . . The office also worked closely with the White House Iraq Group, whose high-level members, including recently indicted Cheney chief of staff Lewis Libby, were responsible for selling the war to the American public.
>
> Never before in history had such an extensive secret network been established to shape the entire world's perception of a war. "It was not just bad intelligence—it was an orchestrated effort," says Sam Gardner, a retired Air Force colonel who has taught strategy and military operations at the National War College. "It began before the war, was a major effort during the war and continues as post-conflict distortions."

Curiously, this type of thing just seems to keep happening again and again.

For example, there was neoconjuror Judith Miller, the weapons of mass destruction expert for the *New York Times*, and her really-barely-a-connection-at-all-really connections to the Pentagon's Office of Special Projects (OSP), a *very* special office within the Pentagon created by Paul Wolfowitz and Douglas Feith.

It was a good idea to invent this very special office.

Those boys needed intelligence, and the CIA was too grumpy to do it right. Your administration didn't trust the sly old CIA to come up with the goods on WMDs. The OSP was created to be an *alternative* CIA—one more *helpful* to the administration's goals of declaring war on Iraq.

Now let's play ring-around-the-acronym:

Judith Miller got her WMD information from Ahmed Chalabi, a helpful Iraq insider on the Pentagon payroll, and the Iraqi National Congress (INC)—an organization founded and named by none other than John Rendon (who later helped install Chalabi as head of the INC). Miller printed her (later discredited) articles in the *New York Times*; the OSP then used Miller's articles as evidence that Iraq had WMDs. The OSP supported the WMD findings of the INC and vice versa. You may be asking yourself, "WTF?"

Simply put, they were all rolling around in bed together, and they basically just invented the whole thing. Miller went to jail impersonating a principled journalist to prevent her whole klatsch of pals from being exposed to charges of "policy fixing," and the rest is a gravel vacant lot overseas somewhere, with a bunch of oil under it. We like oil.

Boom!

Then there was the recent Pentagon pundit scandal, wherein virtually all America's major TV networks were using—as unbiased "military analyst" pundits—Pentagon-approved retired generals and admirals who were in fact utilized by the Pentagon as "message multipliers": good ol' boys willing to parrot the administration's talking points, and flatter the administration and show bobblehead-style support for its foreign policy.

From the front-page *New York Times* story on the scandal (which was very lonely because it was not picked up as a major story by any other major news organization): "Records and interviews show how the Bush administration has used its control over access and information in an effort to transform the [military] analysts into a kind of media Trojan horse—an instrument intended to shape terrorism coverage from inside the major TV and radio networks."

The supposed reason why the story didn't get picked up by other mainstream news agencies lay in the fact that the conflict of interest was a little bit *fuzzy*. True, the pundits received no *direct* payola from the Pentagon, but there was inestimable *indirect* payoff in the liminal nethersphere of access to key figures in the Department of Defense—like Donald Rumsfeld.

Which is great if you happen to be on the board of directors of, say, a private military-industrial corporation and your company is trying to sell contracts to the Pentagon.

The private sector of the defense industry essentially provides the de facto retirement benefits for high-level military men—the golden parachute for silvered paratroopers. After years of hard work and sacrifice for modest pay, they finally get to cash in, in their later careers, as "consultants"—i.e., sit around on boards of directors, provide expertise and oversee studies for private industry. It is inestimably important that these old soldiers get cozy with key figures in the Pentagon whose camaraderie can help their companies get massive, sick, lucre-rich contracts with the Department of Defense. Access is a critical component to landing these gargantuan contracts, particularly under an administration that consistently rewards loyalty and complicity above anything else, including actual skill or experience.

But really, we must consider the plight of the poor retired military pundits in this matter.

Retired generals and admirals are cripplingly vain, and this is used *against* them. The Pentagon exploits their pathetic eagerness to display their plumage and expertise. TV punditry is irresistible ego-Viagra for the over-the-hill warrior chieftains. These retired military men get to feel vital and necessary and be the center of attention again. All the Pentagon wants from them is their loyalty, and, in return, it is friendly and receptive to pitches from their companies. Everyone is happy (except, perhaps, for the irritated hippies who are unemployable enough to become upset about the fact that the American public was manipulated into an inestimably costly and protracted war).

Anyway, how does one legally quantify "influence"? How does one put a price on "friendship"?

How can one overestimate the value of being in the right frat house?

Tss. There's no *conspiracy*.

That would mean somebody was actually in *charge*.

I give you my solemn oath as a Holy Roman American that nobody's in charge now, and nobody ever will be.

There is no "there" here.

There is merely a loose coalition of mutually interested parties with no mastermind. The dragon has no brain. There is no master plan, just a lot of similarly hypnotized chickens.

And as you well know, thousands of years ago, a dragon and a chicken were the same thing.

In this ongoing battle to win your hearts and minds, we must pause for a moment to show appreciation for the bravery of the White House press secretaries. They truly are the thin pinstripe line protecting the American public from clarity.

The James S. Brady Press Briefing Room at the White House is truly where fantasy becomes reality.

A White House press secretary shoulders the difficult task of standing before the free press of the United States—the cream of American journalism—and *never telling them anything substantially informative, ever.*

Your White House press secretary is your undertaker of information. With the gentle sterility of a mortician, he or she puts on a dark suit every day and tells America, in a soothing voice, how comfortable her beloved information will be now that it is dead.

Sadly, the truth is in heaven, and America will never see it again. The press secretary understands your grief, but getting angry won't bring it back.

In order to keep frustrated journalists engaged in a state of passive cooperation, group mania, and active participation in guaranteeing their own dismay and obsolescence (a state of learned helplessness also found in victims of ritualized abuse), the press secretary must be exceptionally skilled at delivering briefings in a highly choreographed, content-free, postmodern language jiu-jitsu. This simulates a psychological thrill similar to one of those groups of bolted seats on a moving floor at the amusement park, where a film is shown that creates a vague sensation of propulsion but actually nothing is really going anywhere, at all.

White House press secretary Dana Perino, for example, is a true master of this Orwellian cage fight.

Ms. Perino may look like a simple party-line-whining trophy blonde in Easy Spirit footwear, but she is actually a fearsome Robo-Shrew, housing a writhing cluster of giant, bloodsucking space-eels. No doubt she speaks eight languages, runs fourteen miles a day, plays classical violoncello, eats nothing but spelt, pennies and thumbtacks, does splits in any direction and excretes .600 Nitro caliber bullets on cue.

She's Vesuvius-hot. She's Bilderberg Barbie. She probably puts polonium 210 in her matcha green tea latte every morning, and it only makes her *stronger*.

I believe she is an emanation of Prosperina, Queen of the Dead, and would no doubt be a gifted poisoner. With a bit of practice, I am sure she can turn civilians into pillars of salt with her seething, napalm-eyed scowl and Rovian mind-needles.

If any major player in this administration is ever kidnapped by al-Qaeda and tortured for national secrets, we can only hope that it is Dana Perino. Like a quality linoleum, Dana will never crack.

I will appoint Dana Perino as undersecretary for public diplomacy—not because I think she will convert hearts and minds by convincing Muslim women they want to be American, but just for a new reality show I am pitching called *I, Miss America*:

Dana gets dropped in the Ysyk-Köl Oblasty of Kazakhstan wearing a lot of jewelry and a white pantsuit, and is forced to take refuge in a cave with some old women with no teeth and tattooed foreheads, who ululate curses and throw chicken entrails at her until she becomes their maidservant and learns to make yak-felt.

I can already feel the advertising billions flying in.

Ryan Seacrest, because of his startling inability to ever look sincere saying anything, shall be given the honor of being my White House press secretary and imperial deceptionist.

Ryan would be able to shrug off any national disaster: "How tr-r-rragic. Anything after so many untimely deaths seems trivial . . . but there are other stories today! . . . There's a new Kim Kardashian sex tape . . ."

I believe that Ryan, more than any previous White House press secretary, has the blue-white teeth, smug disapproval, sneevy nonchalance, boredom and mind-blowing banality that would truly drive all serious reporters into purple fits of vengeance and rage.

And so, to enhance Americans' enjoyment of their new White House press secretary, Ryan will be forced to wear an electric canine shock-collar. Members of the press corps who believe Ryan is lying or merely insufferable will be allowed to punish him physically from the comfort of their seats with small electric buttons installed for this purpose.

Drip, drip. Zap! Zap!

Win-win.

And so, the Mighty Wurlitzer plays on. Now it's accompanied by a whole new bunch of Garage Band–type, greasy kid instruments; cheaper, dirtier little Wurlitzers. And the music just keeps getting louder.

4

DIVUS CALIGULUS: NEO-CAESAROPAPISM, AMERICAN STYLE

Herod put on a garment made wholly of silver, and
of a truly wonderful contexture . . . The silver of
his garment was illuminated by the fresh reflection
of the sun's rays upon it. It shone out after a surprising manner, and was so resplendent as to
spread a horror over those that looked intently
upon him. At that moment, his flatterers cried out . . .
that he was a god; and they added, "Be thou
merciful to us; for although we have hitherto reverenced thee only as a man, yet shall we henceforth
own thee as superior to mortal nature."
Upon this the king did neither rebuke them, nor
reject their impious flattery.

—Flavius Josephus

No man with a good car needs to be justified.

—Hazel Motes, in *Wise Blood* by Flannery O'Connor

Another way in which the American presidency really hasn't gone far enough is this whole "divinely chosen by God" schtick.

American presidents have been indulging a lot of flirtatious edge-play when it comes to having a state religion, but again, there have been failures of imagination and will. Your presidents haven't been scepters-and-balls-to-the-wall enough in this regard. I argue that an imperial cult of personality is just as natural a part of the death spiral of an empire as unsustainable territorial expansion, or matricide!

It is my intention that your future American president really start walking the God's-highest-infallible-representative-on-Earth walk.

I mean, *really*: If it's "holiness elevated beyond the laws of man" you're selling, you *at least* need to wear a gold-lamé suit and a big-ass pinky ring, if not a really tall hat.

Suetonius wrote that the last words of Emperor Vespasian were *puto deus fio* ("I think I'm turning into a god").

I think these should have been the *first* words of Vespasian when taking office.

Oho, you think I'm the only one who built and dedicated temples of worship to myself while serving as emperor?

Julius Caesar started that whole shell game, in my family. The same year he declared himself "Dictator for Life," he OK'd the building of a statue of himself with the inscription "Deo Invicto"—"to the unconquered God."

It became very convenient for everyone in my family that Julius was suddenly a god, because that meant that his descendants, too, were omnipotently leaderish by birth, no matter how unqualified and/or brain damaged we were. Augustus, who had been adopted by Julius, milked this for all it was worth by building a temple to "Divus Julius"—the *divine* Julius, thank you very much—thereby kick-starting the imperial cult tradition of apotheosis, otherwise known as "declaring yourself the de facto Holy Baby Jesus by officially making your dead predecessor/parent God."

The imperial cults were a cushy deal, at least until Constantine I started seeing golden cups in the sky and a meteor hit his battlefield—which frightened him into enough of a shrieking, apron-wringing panic to convert to Christianity and thereby punk out a truly fab and useful tradition. (What a *whimp*.)

But it wasn't like there weren't fiercely dominant religious authorities in town after that. Byzantine Caesaropapism definitely had its charms . . . if you were Charlemagne and part of his whole Carolingian dynasty. The Holy Roman Empire crew had a *very* cushy relationship with the papacy (at least until the whole tenth-century pornocracy thing—but what's a handful of corrupt papacies, more or less, when there's so many to choose from?).

In any case, the "state trumps church" rule really beats the gold brocade dress off of "church ruling state," at least from the dealer's point of view. And it wasn't just for Czar Ivan the Terrible or societies that threw virgins down wells and believed in the spontaneous generation of eels. Caesaropapism was large and in charge in Turkey until 1923 and in Cyprus until Archbishop Makrios stepped down in 1977, and those societies could almost be considered *civilized.*

Machiavelli considered most ruling authorities too superstitious to properly abuse religious authority, which is why he had such admiration for the Borgias. They really knew how to blow the stack out of a pope hat, money-shot style.

Rodrigo Borgia—essentially the Tony Soprano of his day—bought the papacy and became Pope Alexander VI, who, Machiavelli commented, was "of all the pontiffs there have ever been, the first to show what a pope with money and troops could do."

For starters, Alexander let his son Cesare kill his older son Juan and then run around subordinating other parts of Italy with the papal army, then completely absolved himself from the fact that either he or Cesare impregnated his daughter Lucrezia. Nobody could remember who did what or when in that nonstop blur of papal orgies, and that's because nobody cared, because things were different in those days—being God's select representative on Earth meant having *actual earthly power.*

Then there were the Medicis, who were the papal *bankers*, for crying out loud. Right on top of their banking ledgers was the slogan "In the Name of God and Profit" (which was at least refreshingly honest).

When Giovanni de' Medici became Pope Leo X, he told his brother Giulio (who later became the equally fabulous Pope Clement VII), "Since God has given us the papacy, let us enjoy it."

Leo X then commenced enjoying said papacy with a Michael Jackson–ian level of shopaholism and a

Dubai-casino VIP-level lifestyle beyond his means, which included a white elephant named Hanno and other indulgences that he couldn't sell indulgences and cardinal's hats fast enough to pay for. Toward the end, he had to pawn everything: palace furniture, jewelry, silverware and religious statuary, to pay off debts enormous enough to take several banks and rich friends down with him when he died—which is really impressive when you consider that this was some four-hundred-plus years before the invention of free-basing.

What I'm trying to say is that it's not like history ever really had a shortage of nasty Holy Emperors. Like bell-bottoms and medieval torture techniques, they may go under the radar for a while, but they keep coming back.

But nobody ever doubts who is in charge. Being a leader who is remembered throughout history is about making a *strong and lasting impression.*

Take that wacky modern cannibal Jean-Bédel Bokassa. He proclaimed himself imperial majesty of the Central African Empire with a twenty-million-dollar coronation in 1977 (at which the prankster was said to have fed international delegates the flesh of schoolchildren). His divinity didn't last very long, but oh, what a fashion comeback for the flowing ermine robe (which we all thought was such a cliché that it was relegated solely to Playmobil figurines at that point). My point is, how many other African leaders' names can you remember (not including Idi Amin)?

I propose a new Holy American order. I am loosely calling it PresidentioPapism.

Here's the plan: We completely abolish all notions of secularity in government, corporations and military authority and make the American president the number-one Sky God of the one big unifying church to eat all others.

Everything from the regulation of NBA tube socks to the enslavement of Bolivians will be "faith based" and therefore controlled under one huge compulsory federal religion.

One nation, under ME.

Supreme Over-Commander of All Force Whatsoever, Both Real and Imaginary.

Amen.

Think of it as the imperial cult, American style . . . with an attitude!

Just saying you were chosen by God is weak. Saying you *are* The God and making sure that each and every citizen fears you, has a statue of you in the house and makes regular sacrifices to you? This really sexes-up the empire.

Machiavelli said it best: "Ecclesiastical princes alone can hold states without defending them, and subjects without governing them."

Faith is the ultimate imperial tool! By all means, if you're planning on being an emperor, give your slave-class peons the gift of religion. That way, they'll have a standard of perfection to live up to, enforced by their own families and communities, and they'll moderate their own behavior to avoid a crippling sense of shame and inadequacy.

"There is a road to freedom. Its milestones are Obedience, Endeavor, Honesty, Order, Cleanliness,

Sobriety, Truthfulness, Sacrifice, and love of the Fatherland." Those are the wholesome words of a little-known landscape artist by the name of Adolf Hitler.

"Render unto Caesar that which is Caesar's" is perhaps the most helpful instrument of political control the Bible ever gave us, next to that "turn the other cheek" slogan that enabled my family to kick the living Nazarenes out of generations of Christians without fear of retribution.

It was really too easy.

Give your oppressed masses a sense of virtue accumulated through suffering, and stand back and marvel as they censor themselves and act in a decent, God-fearing, law-abiding and—best of all—*long-suffering* manner, in order to feel ethically superior to you.

I've been at this game a mighty long time.

Take it from me: He who has the occult has the office. In other words: Do, do that voodoo.

In Rome, we had the art of augury and the Sibylline prophecies. We could hardly decide how to pluck our own eyebrows without consulting them, and in awe and trembling conducted elaborate pagan rituals to ward off our toga-wetting fear of comets and other natural disasters. This was helpful and community-building. (Augurs and prophecies were a double-edged sword though. If, say, an owl showed up anywhere near you at a public gathering? You were just *fucked*. Owl? *Fucked*.)

I have it on good authority that Fidel Castro thwarted CIA assassination attempts for years by dousing his own head in the fresh blood of white pigeons. I am told you can't find white pigeons in Cuba anymore, for love or money. (And now look what happened to him. Coincidence?)

The White Houses of Abraham Lincoln and Warren Harding are said to have found guidance in astrology; astrologer-to-the-stars Sydney Omarr once described Richard Nixon and Henry Kissinger as really "gung-ho" about it.

But Ronald Reagan, bless his greasy Alberto V05 pompadour, was the first truly nervous occultist ever to have access to nuclear launch codes.

Reagan, of course, was famously superstitious. He held off press conferences until the moon was full; he wouldn't make big moves while Mercury was in retrograde. While generally regarded as intellectually incurious, Reagan had a keen interest in UFOs and ghosts, and he frequently expressed a somber belief that the foretold signs of Armageddon were lining up.

I intend to take occult in the White House one step further by reinitiating a national religion and rebranding new state gods . . . .

. . . which, fortunately for you, are basically the same as the old state gods!

We Romans originally got our polytheism from the Etruscans. It was a simple animism like most others that arose in primitive cultures: a divine, archetypal middle management to whom we could appeal in order to haplessly convince ourselves that we had some influence over the random cruelties dished out by forces greater than ourselves.

I know forced conversions don't usually go down so well with societies, historically, but I think you're going to like this one. Seriously.

(It's not like I'm not asking you to jump-start chthonic hero cults and sacrifice puppies to Hecate at all crossroads.)

Once you've gotten over your usual fit of riots, be-ins and protests, once the smoke of your neighborhoods clears, we will all agree as Americans that what is most important is that we come together under one, roomy, unifying faith for the sake of joining each other hand in hand in our places of worship and getting down to the real business on the table: the persecution of Scientologists and the confiscating of their extensive property holdings.

You ready for your souls to get shock-rocked? Here it comes.

I have wonderful news: The divine exists and is omnipresent. Gods are present in each and every aspect of your lives. They provide you with pleasure, food, goods, services, intelligence, transportation, weaponry . . . even the gift of flight.

In short, affordable luxury! Right under your noses! The kingdom of heaven is *all around you.* What will you do with all the money you save?

In olden days, we used to place little oil lamps to honor our gods, and anoint ourselves in oils for ceremonies. We had it all backward.

Now here's the surprise: You're already doing it right. Like Ed McMahon used to say, you may already be a winner.

Oil, obviously, is one of the most primary divine movers. So now, accordingly, we offer *ourselves, our blood sacrifices and our gods to oil, instead of the other way around.*

Du-u-u-u-u-u-uh, right?

Needless to say, we live and learn. Fortunately our present leaders have clarified this, and we are no longer the heathen we once were.

After I have my coronation and the Senate declares me pontifex maximus, Americans will be required to make periodic sacrifices to my numens, my genius and my Holy Spirit. In exchange, you will all receive valuable coupons!

Americans are already tithing to their new corporate godheads. That's the beauty and simplicity of it: You're going to become even more empowered by doing exactly what you're already doing—through *faith*.

Fantastic, isn't it? Don't you feel holier already?

Here's what I'm going to do.

First, just like Louis XIV, I will be declared Sol Invictus. All other divine superbrands and federal agencies will rotate in gravitational thrall to me.

Just like Kim Il Sung, I will be Caligula, my next dynastic Caligula will be Caligula, and their subsequent Caligulae will also be Caligula, and we Caligula will always be your divine president, forever and ever, world without end.

I, Caligula, shall rule under the title of

TYRANNO-PRESIDENTIUS OPTIMUS
MAXIMUS REX, or,

HE WHO HAS ABSOLUTE DOMINION OVER
EVERYTHING THAT MOVES, CRAWLS, BREATHES,
GENERATES INCOME OR OTHERWISE EXISTS.

That will kick things off.

Now, I am proud to introduce your new Holy American Superbrands. The "Places of Worship" lists are obviously incomplete, but the clever among you ought to be able to fill in the blanks once you get the gist of it.

Behold.

This is your annunciation. Cower, weep and sing.

TYRANUS©

(Formerly known as JUPITER/ZEUS)

GOD OF POWER, LIGHT AND ENERGY

Oil, the nuclear bomb

PLACES OF WORSHIP
BP
Chevron
ConocoPhillips
Exxon Mobil
Federal Communications Commission (FCC)
Federal Election Commission (FEC)
Federal Energy Regulatory Commission (FERC)
Koch Industries
Nuclear Regulatory Commission (NRC)
Royal Dutch Shell

High Priests: Electrical engineers with Asperger's syndrome

LUCRA©

(Formerly known as JUNO/HERA: QUEEN OF HEAVEN)

GODDESS OF PROSPERITY AND HIGH FINANCE

Gold, diamonds, banks, private equity, hedge funds, stock market

PLACES OF WORSHIP
Bank of America Corporation
Blackstone Group
Credit Suisse Customized Fund Investment Group
Fannie Mae, Freddie Mac
Federal Trade Commission (FTC)
GMAC Financial Services
Goldman Sachs Private Equity Group
ING Group
International Trade Commission (ITC)
PricewaterhouseCoopers
Securities and Exchange Commission (SEC)

AUTOMO©

(Formerly known as APOLLO)

GOD OF AUTOMOTIVE AND SURVEILLANCE INDUSTRIES AND TECHNOLOGIES

He sees you when you're sleeping; he knows when

you're awake. Formerly the god of air and space travel until a recent hostile takeover by **WARIUS©**.

PLACES OF WORSHIP
CIA
DaimlerChrysler
Defense Intelligence Agency (DIA)
European Aeronautic Defence and Space Company (EADS)
FBI
Ford
General Motors (GM)
National Security Agency (NSA)
United Technologies

WARIUS©

(Formerly known as MARS/ARES)

GOD OF THE MILITARY, AEROSPACE INDUSTRIES, THE MILITARY-INDUSTRIAL COMPLEX, PRIVATE SECURITY SERVICES, MERCENARIES

Big Daddy and his big, big guns.

PLACES OF WORSHIP
Barrett
Bechtel
Blackwater
Colt
Defense Advanced Research Projects Agency (DARPA)

Department of Defense
General Electric
Halliburton/KBR
Honeywell International
Lockheed Martin
Northrop Grumman
Raytheon
Triple Canopy

PHARMA©

(Formerly known as ATHENA/MINERVA)

GODDESS OF WISDOM, MEDICINE, SCIENCE AND TECHNOLOGY

Basically, pills.

PLACES OF WORSHIP
Bayer—Germany
GlaxoSmithKline—U.K.
Johnson & Johnson—USA
Pfizer—USA

Offerings: Blood, healthy organs for transplant auctions

Hospitalita©

(Formerly known as VESTA/HESTIA)

GODDESS OF HOME AND HEARTH

Home industries, hotel/hospitality industries, real estate development . . . in short, the spirit of "comfiness."

PLACES OF WORSHIP
Home Depot
Marriott
Wal-Mart

Saint: Oprah

Nutritia©

(Formerly known as CERES/DEMETER)

GODDESS OF AGRIBUSINESS

The Ultimate Oedipal conquest of Mother Nature.

PLACES OF WORSHIP
Altria
Archer Daniels Midland
Cargill
Kraft
Monsanto

Nestlé
Tyson Foods
Ubiquitous food chains (Denny's, McDonald's, Burger King, Dunkin' Donuts, etc.)

Offerings: Gifts of cigarettes, bacon double cheeseburgers, breaded chicken or fish sticks, Big Gulp cups full of nacho cheese

METALLICO©

(Formerly known as VULCAN/HEPHAESTUS)

GOD OF METALS AND RECONSTRUCTION

WARIUS© bombs it down . . . **METALLICO©** rebuilds it!

PLACES OF WORSHIP
Alcoa
Bechtel
Carlyle
Halliburton/KBR
Mittal Steel
Nippon Steel
Norsk Hydro
ThyssenKrupp

MEDIUS©

(Formerly known as MERCURY/HERMES)

GOD OF TELECOMMUNICATIONS, ENTERTAINMENT, MEDIA-INDUSTRIAL COMPLEX

Anything slick and shiny that gets your attention, really.

PLACES OF WORSHIP
AT&T
Bertelsmann
Disney
News Corporation
Sprint Nextel, etc.
Time Warner
Verizon Communications

Narcissa©

(Formerly known as VENUS/APHRODITE)

GODDESS OF BEAUTY AND DIETING INDUSTRIES

The divine science of making women feel old, fat and ugly—then granting them the hope that they can buy their way out of it.

PLACES OF WORSHIP
Avon
Estée Lauder
L'Oréal
Procter & Gamble
Shiseido
Unilever

Offerings: Bulimia, Restylane

BLUTO©

(Formerly known as PLUTO)

GOD OF THE UNDERWORLD

Prison-industrial complex, Mafia, "The Dark Side"

PLACES OF WORSHIP
Cornell Companies
Corrections Corporation of America
The GEO Group (formerly Wackenhut Corrections Corporation)

Offerings: Felonies, tax evasion, televised capture and humiliation on MSNBC under Megan's Law dragnet-style operations

VICE©

(Formerly known as BACCHUS/DIONYSUS)

GOD OF DEBAUCHERY AND HEDONISM

Alcohol, casinos, sex industry, rehab industry: in a word, Fun!

PLACES OF WORSHIP
Dubai
Hedonism II
Ibiza
Las Vegas
Monte Carlo
Qatar

MR. SALTY©

(Formerly known as NEPTUNE/POSEIDON)

GOD OF SHIPPING, FISHING, WATER

Fuck Neptune. I am draining the oceans to make room for better land-development deals. Water is being phased out.

And lastly, a brand-new divine American Superbrand:

MAMMON©

(ANY AND ALL OF THE TOP 100 LARGEST CORPORATIONS ACCORDING TO *FORBES* OR *FORTUNE* MAGAZINE)

Never fear, people. There is a kingdom of heaven.

A Valhalla. A Mount Olympus. Whatever inspirational reward mulches your spiritual lawn. And it's not just "within you" either.

You have Qatar, Dubai, Disneyland, and Las Vegas.

And for those of you who are very, very, very special indeed—saints, if you will, of our new mandatory State Animism—there is a higher goal.

Yes, if you really, really, really behave (and *we are watching*; you are under constant surveillance, thanks to AUTOMO©), you may be elevated bodily into heaven, Rapture-style, and taken to the official ruling-class, Trilateral-Bilderberger-Council-of-Foreign-and-Intergalatic-Relations-sanctioned recreational space-pyramid.

No laws. One-way mirrors, glass-bottomed hot tubs, hyperbaric opium chambers, vodka waterslide.

I can't say more or my friends will shoot me. Suffice to say that if you have to ask, you can't even think about it.

But it's there. Trust me.

I know when you've been bad or good, and if you're really good, you'll be picked up by a platinum rocket ship, right in front of all your friends at work, and given a full joy ride of inexpressible heavenly bliss.

Because I love you.

In fact, I love you so much I am giving you a whole new zodiac.

In honor of my glorious regime, the months of the year will now be changed to reflect both American world domination and your enduring love for my divine leadership. The renaming of months will naturally also necessitate a revamping of corresponding astrological signs.

Introducing the newer, better, hipper i-Zodiac! (i-Zod.) Think of it as your Zodiac 2.0!

Those born in the corresponding months will surely find themselves amazed to reflect these "typical" characteristics!

January shall be KNOWN HENCEFORTH AS CHENEYUARY.
i-Zod: RIFLE, Sign of the PIONEER
Pros: Stealth, cunning, domination
Cons: Rancor, deceit, constant threat of sudden death

Feburary shall be KNOWN HENCEFORTH AS PFIZER.
i-Zod: VIAGRUS, Sign of the STALLION
Pros: Virility, fecundity
Cons: Aggression, rape

March, formerly in honor of the Roman god Mars, shall be KNOWN HENCEFORTH AS BOEING.
i-Zod: RAPTOR, Sign of the F-22

Pros: Strength, indomitability, lethality
Cons: Ineptitude, spendoholism, planned obsolescence

April shall be KNOWN HENCEFORTH AS EPCOT.
i-Zod: DISNEY, Sign of the FRANCHISE
Pros: Ubiquity, adorableness, piety
Cons: Immaturity, pandering, diabetes

May shall now be NAMED MICROSOFT.
i-Zod: TOP HAT, Sign of the MONOPOLY
Pros: Wealth, mathematical ability, altruism
Cons: Social anxiety, Asperger's syndrome–like behaviors, physical weakness

June shall now be NAMED YALE.
i-Zod: FRATTO, Sign of the LEGACY
Pros: Pride, wealth, Machiavellian tendencies
Cons: Insecurity, smugness, gender-confusion issues

July shall, for a probationary period, be KNOWN AS JOLIE.
i-Zod: UBIQUITA, Sign of the CELEBRITY
Pros: Eroticism, altruism, wealth
Cons: Melancholia, procreational greed, ballbusting

August, previously named for Emperor Augustus, shall now be KNOWN AS CALIGULA REX.
i-Zod: MUFASA, Sign of the LION KING
Pros: Indomitability, conspicuous consumption, elitism
Cons: Amorality, addictive tendencies, malignant narcissism, antisocial pathologies

September IS now two months long, and named BARBRA.
i-Zod: REGINA, Sign of the DOWAGER EMPRESS
Pros: Domination, thrift, chastity, talent, ability to inspire fear
Cons: Prudishness, contextual dissonance, morbid narcissism, bulk

October shall now be KNOWN AS RAYTHEON.
i-Zod: THAAD, Sign of the TERMINAL HIGH ALTITUDE AREA DEFENSE RADAR SYSTEM
Pros: Intelligence, surveillance, reconnaissance
Cons: Nihilism, tyranny, genocide

November shall be ELIMINATED ENTIRELY, to help heal the national malaise that has long surrounded the (now happily obliterated) bipartisan scourge of voting.

December, the Holy Month, will BE RENAMED SANTA-CLAS, and devoted entirely to the purchasing and bringing of devotional gifts exclusively to the Chosen Occupants of the White House.
i-Zod: ROLEX, Sign of QUALITY WORKMANSHIP
Pros: Luster, conspicuous consumption, exclusivity
*Cons: Vacuity, moral ambivalence, white-collar crime**

---

*Citizens displaying any ongoing reverence for the pagan idolatry of the previous, now defunct astrology will be brought to trial on charges of Sorcery, a misdemeanor punishable by fines of up to $3,000. Please tune in to local Fox-affiliated news stations to be informed of your local calendar and hard drive bonfires. All previous calendars, both personal and digital, shall be rendered null and void, now and in perpetuity. Possession shall be punishable by a $5,000 fine or six years incarceration.

In conclusion, let me summarize by saying this: The Kingdom of Heaven: Get it in you. It's the law.

Amen.

5

A DEMOCRACY BY ANY OTHER NAME WOULD STILL BE THE OLDEST, MOST CLASSIC EXCUSE FOR BEATING YOU UP AND TAKING YOUR STUFF

The 20th century has been characterized by three developments of great political importance: The growth of democracy, the growth of corporate power, and the growth of corporate propaganda as a means of protecting corporate power against democracy.
—Alex Carey, social scientist

Democracy means simply the bludgeoning of the people by the people for the people.
—Oscar Wilde

Democracy is only a dream: it should be put in the same category as Arcadia, Santa Claus, and Heaven.
—H. L. Mencken

There never was a democracy yet that
did not commit suicide.
—John Adams

Many theoretical politicians the world over
confidently expect modern democracies to
throw themselves at the feet of some Caesar.
—Woodrow Wilson

While you're down there, polish my stun baton.
—Gaius Caligula

I've got one for ya:

Q: *When is a democracy not a democracy?*
A: *Always.*

(Hahahahaha. No, just kidding. Your vote totally "counts.")

Woodrow Wilson said he thought all political systems inevitably guttered out, in the end, into a democracy.

Anyone who's been around the historical block a few times knows that democracies tend to mutate into either empires or anarchies, both of which devolve quite handily into tyrannies, and all of which ultimately decompose into authoritarian military dictatorships.

You may whine all you like, but I can't guarantee your safety afterward.

I prefer to think that America is moving away from the stagnant democracy it has been mired in, according to stodgy, literal, Borkian interpretations of ancient documents like the Constitution (which is as risible as any literal interpretation of any document from the New Testament to *The Hobbit*), and moving into something truly exciting: a more Rabelaisian, "carnivalesque" democracy—something I am loosely calling

Democracy Extremo-MAXX!

(It's basically . . . tyranny, but we're not going to call that spade a spade because that would be politically incorrect and demoralize the republic.)

It has been said that civilizations are subject to natural catastrophes that force them to revert back to their barbarous beginnings. (Natural catastrophes, military overthrows, sack-and-pillage—same diff.)

Let's wander a considerable distance backward down memory lane.

The citizens of Rome were craving a mild and reasonable leadership after years of getting their tongues pulled out under the monarchic whim of Etruscan tyrants. So, around 509 B.C., they kick-started the SPQR: *Senatus Populusque Romanus*. The Roman Republic, "the Senate and the People of Rome."

Rome had a constitution; our senate was the chief and most powerful branch of government. Its members made all the foreign policy and had complete control of the treasury—wars, therefore, couldn't be declared without the senate's approval.

It was boring and lame. Since 95 percent of Romans lived below the poverty line, elections were naturally rigged in favor of the rich (because poor people weren't raised by aristocrats and were therefore tacky and untrustworthy).

In any case, all SPQR pretenses of reasonableness came to a screaming halt when a natural catastrophe named Julius conquered Gaul, crossed the Rubicon with his legions, enacted a hostile takeover, declared himself Dictator for Life and proceeded to consolidate all the power he could collect and centralize it right into his own jock.

This wasn't taken as a patriotic thing to do. Brutus and few other jealous, pissy big-nylon-toga-wearing grandmas in the senate started wagging their loose upper-arm flesh into a flightless lather about reanimating the Republic. Julius was assassinated, and *blah blah blah* ancient history.

But, despite their little murder, the senators' plans turned to dung. Civil war broke out for a couple of years, and finally Octavian, Julius's adopted son, became Augustus Caesar—the first official Roman emperor, dynastic-monarchy-style. And in an ultimate smackdown for republican sentiment, as we discussed earlier, Julius was officially declared a god, ho ho ho.

And here's where things began to get murky, because here's where subtle domestic propaganda really kicked into overdrive.

Augustus established the Principate—a weird phase in Rome, during which a lot of dog and pony shows were still enacted for the citizenry in order to pretend that Rome was still kinda-sorta a republic, even though it was really a whole lot more like a constitutional monarchy and kinda-sorta state religious cult.

Oh sure, there was still a constitution, and still a senate, in theory. But Augustus named himself the "princeps," or the "First Citizen"—meaning, "Hey, kids, I am a 'citizen' just exactly like each and every one of you very important people (only actually I am exponentially more important and therefore Bossman Numero Uno and you aren't)."

The imperial spin was that the emperor wasn't a swinging, debonair autocrat with his patent-leather tuxedo pump standing on your face at all; he was the nation's virtuous dad—an ideal, mature, just and merciful guy, like Fred MacMurray in *My Three Sons*—only with an actual dick, and an army. But still wearing a neutered-looking cardigan and projecting an aura of benevolent reasonableness and clemency, instead of out-and-out killer sexiness.

But that's *right*. You *shouldn't* think of your emperor as your supreme overlord. Instead, think of him as the nice paternal guy who controls your life for your own protection and makes tough decisions for the whole family (since you, the average citizens, are basically incompetent, childlike half-men, three-holed livestock and/or incarcerated).

The Principate ruse went on for a while with everyone sort of almost believing they were living under something other than a dynastic monarchy, until the third-century crisis of 235 to 284, when the army proclaimed Diocletian, who was a real one-man costume drama of a bull-whipping crypto-sadist, the emperor.

Diocletian was not into being a "princeps." This was not kinky enough. He wanted the citizenry to get down and suck the glove.

Diocletian started the Dominate (cue ominous movie-trailer kettle drums). He declared himself the *dominus*—translation "master."

The subjects were, therefore, literally, "servus," or slaves.

Spank. Me. Daddy.

Anyway, like any good autocrat, Diocletian had a real flair for the bold theatrics of tyranny.

He came right out with the gold Cadillac, royal crown, heavy cocktail jewelry and swanky purple garments, and let the Roman people know exactly how embitchified they were with massive "fuck you, I'm Imperial" architecture—just to really jackhammer home how uncrossably wide the ravine between emperors and peons was.

Really lucky trailer-class suckers were sometimes allowed to prostrate themselves and kiss the hem of Diocletian's robe. (I used to make my subjects do that too, but more as a *joke*.)

Anyway, this is part of how my experience as both Caesar and drag entertainer would make me an ideal American president. Nobody born human is actually *qualified* for this job, so naturally it requires some, ahem . . . illusions. Mass hypnosis. Towering prosceniums and country western wigs.

Whether you're an emperor, a president, Wayne Newton or the lead singer of a Swedish death metal band, you are really missing the point of captivating your audience if you are pretending to be on the same scavenger level of humanity as them. Chummy down-to-earthness may make you lovable, but it doesn't inspire awe and trembling (I am naturally excluding the power of immortal global *Hospitalita*© brands, and Oprah).

Let's face it: It's all about increasing the public's terror of your Angry Flaming Head with mirrors, deafening Marshall stacks, smoke flares and firepots. Then, you keep the tension cooking by *re-e-e-eally* gently sliding in the slick Soviet mindwarp, i.e., rewriting current events to reflect your ideal version of them. (This keeps everyone slightly jittery and off-kilter because they have no idea what's really going on or where north is anymore in terms of ontological truth or reality. It's awesome.)

What I'm getting at is that America, right now, is in the awkward phase of its imperial puberty—that wacky, sticky, spurting period of transition. America the adolescent Principate is finally growing pubic hair, having its bar mitzvah, putting on its toga virilis (its "manly gown") and becoming a big, ugly, awkward, volcano-faced Dominate.

Believe me, I know how difficult it is to transition from being the precocious, lovable, childlike upstart Principate nation to being an insufferable, repellant, obese and hateful teenage Dominate in a black T-shirt.

Nobody wants to admit they're a Dominate. Let's face it, the whole oriental, absolute-monarchic-dictatorship thing is just frankly depressing. It's true: The whole Byzantine era was just one big limp, sodden downer. When your government stops bothering to lie to you, it seems like they just don't *care*. It's like letting the White House lawn turn brown and walking out to press conferences with a bottle of Seagram's gin 'n' juice, wearing a polar fleece housecoat streaked with Egg Beaters and a shower cap and screaming unintelligible obscenities into the microphone. It gives You People the impression that your dictator isn't even *trying*.

I say American presidents need to act out their messiah complexes in the bedroom, where they belong, stop worrying about being loved so much, put on the fingerless leather gloves and really get down to the creepy business of becoming the New Improved Holy World Order.

Yes, it's a sadomasochistic power dynamic, and it's a shock, at first, to see your president wearing the black rubber hood out on a Sunday afternoon. It makes the citizenry very jumpy when the puppet show stops and the carnies break the stage down and put their cigarettes out in Humpty Dumpty's eye. But the show must close; night must fall, and so must the empire.

When I was a child, I spake as a child. But when I am your Divine Robo-Emperor, I promise not to insult your intelligence with pretensions of decency.

Realpolitik is not for the twee. If you really want to understand how worlds corrode, you have to look at the fragile web of interconnected personal relationships in top cabinet positions.

I learned a lot about political life as a child growing up in Syria. Not from my father, Germanicus, so much, but from Gnaeus Calpurnius Piso, Emperor Tiberius's governor of Syria, who, apparently under the direction of Tiberius and his mother, murdered my father over a period of months, through a combination of psychological torture, black magic and poison.

And who could blame them. Tiberius was a deeply frightened old catamite, and no doubt felt threatened by the public's love for my handsome war-hero father, Germanicus, and was certainly encouraged in this fretful envy by his mother, Livia, the Mother of Rome and All Battle-axes—Germanicus's grandmother and my great-grandmother. (I used to call her "Ulysses in Petticoats." Today, I'd call her "Idi Amin in Crotchless Vinyl Support Hose.")

Livia, it must be said, did everything a stage mother could do to lethally cock-block all the other heirs apparent to her husband, Emperor Augustus, and divert the tide of history to favor the accession of Tiberius. Back then, good imperial parenting still meant murdering your child's competitors, and in this regard, Livia was practically a one-woman Mouseketeer factory.

Behold how good I am at this game.

In the year 31, I found myself getting invited to visit Emperor Tiberius on the isle of Capri—the Ibiza of the time: a writhing hotbed of narcotic ambrosias, discotheques, nude sunbathing and sexually transmitted diseases. This was a spectacular coup for Yours Truly.

Tiberius was on Capri because the prefect of his Praetorian Guard, Lucius Aelius Sejanus, had been stoking his paranoia by constantly suggesting that there were assassination plots against him, the majority of which existed exclusively in the fungal imagination of Sejanus, who got off on bringing charges of treason and conspiracy down on anyone in Rome who looked at him sideways—like my mom, Agrippina, and my brother, Nero, whom he declared "public enemies" and banished to the Laundromat-size island of Pandateria. (Sejanus also happened to be fucking the wife of Tiberius' son, Drusus, which was handy, because it made it easier to convince her to poison Drusus to death.)

Anyway, Sejanus had a virtual maximum-security, orange-alert lockdown on Rome, and he was having a field day.

But Tiberius didn't want to hear anything bad about Sejanus. Tiberius wasn't an affable guy—basically the Richard Nixon of the Julio-Claudians, given to the boorish habit of distributing spies around the city to eavesdrop on dinner-party conversations, and subsequently punishing people for anything off-color they might have said about him while drunk.

Sejanus gave Tiberius the desperately needed illusion of loyal friendship, and in return, Tiberius pussed over a shocking amount of authority to the guy.

(This has always been a splendid dirty trick beloved of empires and mobsters, and it's a wonder Tiberius wasn't more hip to it: the racket known as "throw a scare into your mark until he begs you to protect him, then gradually get him to trust you and give more and more of his power over to you, then make his world smaller and smaller until he is an entirely punked-out, anxiety-shredded dishrag, imprisoned and at your mercy."

It's a sick little gambit but it works great for kidnappings, cults, extortionists, abusive love affairs and police states. Ahhh . . . the Patriot Act—it's sort of the legislative equivalent of the all-meat diet that becomes popular every forty years under a different name.)

The dead gorilla under the rug that nobody was discussing was the fact that since Tiberius was basically half drunk the whole time, the Praetorian guards under Sejanus were getting way too powerful, and there really wasn't a whole lot besides the guard's conventional *idea of loyalty to the emperor* preventing Sejanus from clotheslining Tiberius and seizing power for himself. They were just one teensy psychological paradigm shift away from the whole military-dictatorial tamale.

It was anybody's guess as to which way the loyalties of the guard would have swung if that had happened. Most of the soldiers, after all, couldn't really give two petrified ostrich balls whose imperial mud flaps were disgracing the throne as long as they could keep their jobs.

Anyway, say what you will about scabby old Tiberius; my time with him on Capri taught me a lot of crucially important leadership tips.

Number one: World leaders have no interest in standing around, looking crap-stained by the light of your lovely moral example. Never expose your superiors to excess decency or ethical standards higher than their own. Instead, do whatever you can to discover, share and overindulge in any vice they might enjoy, and try to discreetly supply your superior with the transgressions he craves.

Extol the leader's virtue and temperance while

cheerfully lamenting the fact that you are an incorrigibly guilty, skulking clot of shame, far more enslaved to the beguilements of shaved goats or German dwarf excrement or (insert their perversion-of-choice here) than they are.

This really got my foot in the imperial door.

Uncle Tiberius and I were bonding over some uproariously nauseating scrolls of Etruscan pornography on Capri when he draped his splotchy, sagging arm around me and said, "Caligula, you shall be my heir."

I provided Tiberius with exactly what he wanted in a successor: a monster even more demented and less qualified for the throne than he was, who, he thought, would make his reign look considerably better by comparison.

Number two: As emperor, you can be paranoid, corrupt, sadistic, drunk and incompetent, as long as you have a lot of very rich friends, a ridiculously aggressive approach to spin control and a highly fortified and corruptible private army.

In other words, just because I was named Tiberius's heir doesn't mean I was out of the woods.

Enter Naevius Sutorius Macro, another prefect of the Praetorian Guard. My deus ex machina.

One might go so far as to say that Macro was something of a proto-example of the truism that as long as there has been civilian leadership, the military has always had a perverse fist in influencing it somehow.

Macro was a climber—I know this because he let me fuck his wife, which was handy because a) I got to fuck his wife, and b) it gave me an excuse to bring a pandering charge against him later. Macro was indispensable in arranging the fall of Sejanus, and was later indispensable in smothering Tiberius, who had annoyed me extremely by remaining alive for too long.

Macro, shall we say, bumped up the pace of events a bit, that I might assume my rightful place as emperor in a timely manner and get down to business.

Oh, don't look so *shocked.* Tiberius was barely functional, pissing away an endless dotage on Capri. His death was a foregone conclusion, and the means by which it was achieved were anything but relevant. This type of thing happens every single minute in your very own nursing homes all over the country and don't pretend it doesn't. *And don't pretend you aren't glad it does.*

Anyway, for Macro's extreme acts of opportunism, ass-kissery and slavish obedience, I allowed him and his impish party favor of a spouse to kill themselves (instead of, say, having them be publicly gored by rhinos).

To give your life for your emperor, after all, is the soldier's most noble profession. These guys love this stuff, bless them. I secretly think they like it even a *little bit better* when they feel that the emperor has personally betrayed them and they get to check out in an ecstatic lather of noble outrage and moral superiority.

In summary, my dear children: Democracy is usually just the way a military dictatorship dresses up in women's clothes from time to time and feels pretty.

If it's macho role-playing costume drama you want, kids . . . . ho ho, I am an old trouper. And we're talking Hellenistic drama here when theater really meant something cathartic—not just oinking around in a Lycra bodystocking and papier-mâché Disney mask.

Aristotle had no great love for democracy. He considered it deviant. Kings, or monarchies, in the process of regime decay, invariably become tyrants. Aristocracies—small groups of virtuous leaders—rot into oligarchies: the rule of wealthy property owners (who invariably believe that the poor are morally corrupt and dog-level inferior).

Aristotle thought democracy was just a corruption of "polity"—the rule by many citizens (but actually only the white males). Democracy, by Aristotle's definition, was something to be assiduously avoided: tyranny of the majority—meaning, rule by the average dipshit stadium yutz. Government by mob.

Yes, it's true: Corrupt governments have the common interests in mind while bad governments serve themselves. But they all turn bad in the end if they hang around long enough.

You Americans jabber endlessly about whether things are "constitutional" or "unconstitutional." These arguments in themselves are pointless because they're completely leapfrogging the core issue: whether or not Americans actually *want* a democracy.

Let me let you in on a little secret. You *don't.*

The vast majority of you (and democracy is, after all, "majority rule") don't actively participate in, protect, fight for or even *understand* democracy. That's perfectly natural, mainly because you've never really *had* a democracy. What you have here, technically, is an oligarchy dressed down and slumming around in the hooded sweatshirt and baggy jeans of democracy.

In short, right now, politically speaking, America is Vanilla Ice.

How do you know an oligarchy when you see one?

Um, the campaign finance system, for one, which pretty much ensures that only squillionaires can play ball.

There are plenty of other oligarchic symptoms going around though. Nepotism. Men ruling the nation instead of laws.

Superdelegates, invariably white and male, whose votes count for approximately ten thousand of yours and who are under no obligation to reflect your political desires and support the candidate you actually want. Blah blah blah. Convinced yet? No matter.

I'll be straight with you: If you want a real regime (and I do), you take "We the People" out of the equation by rephrasing it as "You People," and then remove "You People" as a political actor.

The thing is, You People don't really want to be political actors. What you really want is for your actors to be politicians!

You want John Wayne to be your *dad*. This is perfectly OK and understandable! Similar national tendencies have led to the rise of some of our greatest despots.

It's what you're *supposed* to want.

It's what we *want you* to want.

It's what all our propaganda has worked so hard to *train you* to want.

The really beautiful, magical thing about it is, we train you so superbly well that you actually end up organically wanting it yourself and thinking it was your own idea.

We deform you this way into our ideals of beauty, and they become your own—just as Egyptians, Australian aborigines and Choctaw mothers strapped boards to their children's skulls to make them flatter, or Chinese mothers insisted on stunting their girls' feet like bonsai trees to make them cuter, or other tribespeople cherish freakishly long necks or fan-belt earlobes. You grow up with it all around you, honey—given enough peer pressure, you'll like it too.

So, here's the deal: My private military will take over the government and I will declare a dictatorship, and nothing will really change very much. *Tyranny* is such a dirty word. For a while I thought we should call it "Compassionate Corporate Kick-Ass-ism," but I think it's better, for the next couple of decades, if we just keep calling it a Democracy Extremo-MAXX.

My Democracy Extremo-MAXX is here to serve *you.*

No, wait, I have a better name: Let's call it my Chthonic-Autochthonocracy. And you have to be able to say it ten times fast, or I'll have you killed.

(LOL.)

Father Knows Best.

6

I AM THE WORD, THE LIGHT, THE SUN GOD AND THE LIZARD KING; OR, PLAUSIBLE DENIABILITY—THE REPUBLIC DOES NOT RECALL

No Title of Nobility shall be granted
by the United States.
—U.S. Constitution

The accumulation of all powers, legislative,
executive, and judiciary, in the same hands . . .
is the definition of tyranny.
—James Madison

Whoever is installed as the new guardian of
presidential power will not likely part with many
of the rights that Bush claimed and was
allowed to use, unchallenged.
—Scott Horton, *Harper's*

L'État, c'est moi. (I am the State.)
—Louis XIV

Executive leadership ultimately goes to the candidate wearing the biggest codpiece.

I was elated to become emperor following the death of Tiberius, but I had to get straight to work making sure it actually happened.

Rule number one: *Do* bribe the Praetorian Guard and give them huge bonuses; this ensures their loyalty and is the best way to guarantee your own accession.

The Praetorian prefect Macro, after all, had been my right-hand man in arranging the fall of Sejanus (Tiberius's own black glove, as it were) and in making Tiberius stop breathing. Macro also helped me claim that the part of Tiberius's will that named me joint ruler with his grandson Gemellus was invalid, on the grounds that at the time Tiberius wrote it, he was deranged.

Then Macro helped me get granted the title of imperator by the senate—even though I had obviously never really done anything important, let alone won any great military victories. It didn't matter. This move proved I had the muscle vote: the loyalty of the military commanders and the governors in the provinces.

The message we were sending was very clear and very simple: CRONY PERKS IN THE HOUSE, LIVE AND ON FIRE. TOTAL BUY-IN FOR THE COMPLICIT. FALL IN LOCKSTEP OR ELSE. Back then we used to call what I did with Tiberius (and what Macro did with me) *nihil abnuentum, dum dominationis aspiceretur*, or, "refusing nothing, in the hope of attaining power."

Helloo-oo-oo, all you butch boys in the Pentagon. Yoo-hoo. Hi.

Really, it's just good strategy.

A candidate, after all, is "obliged to sell shares of themselves to the great conglomerates," according to Gore Vidal, who, as a cousin of Jimmy Carter, Al Gore and JFK, ought to know these things.

Gemellus, my co-ruler, on the other hand, didn't understand how power works at all, because Gemellus didn't even have pubic hair.

Honestly, I think Tiberius made me a joint ruler with Gemellus just to fuck with me. I think he wanted to make sure I committed some murder right away, just to kick-start his own legacy of being Not As Bad As Me into high gear right out of the gate.

He had to know that my sharing the throne with Gemellus was about as likely as my sharing the use of my dick with him. The only logical conclusion is that Tiberius didn't really like Gemellus either.

Anyway, as soon as Tiberius was dead, Macro stage-managed my triumphal fifteen-day procession back to Rome from Misenum. You bet your fetishy little boots this is where I seized full advantage of my position as a son of Germanicus and drew heavily on all my talents for drag performance and dramatic spectacle. Word of my procession preceded me along my route. Though I was dressed in mourning and approaching my duty to lead Rome with grim and resolute determination, I looked fucking flawless, and everyone's lives in those suburbs were so completely unfabulous that the raw glamour of the event turned that little turnip patch upside down.

Fans came out with torches and lined the roads to greet me, pissing with ecstasy at the prospect of having a son of Germanicus on the throne, squealing my name like groupies, calling me "baby" and "chick" and "star." Over 160,000 sacrifices were made in my name over the next three months. I was that sexy.

Again, perception really is reality. If you have ever "Obi-Wan Kenobied" your way into a popular nightclub by hypnotizing the bouncer with your Patek Philippe, you are ready for a position of civilian authority.

Once I was in Rome, I realized how fortunate I was that Tiberius had so utterly befouled the bedsheets of the monarchy. Tiberius and Sejanus had made enough enemies that anyone who wasn't Tiberius looked like Madonna by comparison, at least for the first few months.

It was an absolute cakewalk for me to emotionally manipulate the sandals off the senate by sobbing that Tiberius had caused the deaths of my sainted father and my only mother, Agrippina. (I was so shameless I told the senate that I was their "son and ward," and they got all *verklempt*.)

Practically the minute I got into the senate, they fell all over themselves to grant me *ius arbitrium omnium rerum* (power and authority over all things), unbelievably forking over to me all the special magical powers that Augustus had accumulated throughout his forty-one years in office, in one big fat lump sum. Imperial jackpot a-go-go.

My powers were completely off the chain, unlimited by anything but my own colorful, rococo imagination.

The whimpering compliance of the senate at my accession really kicked off progress toward a *lex imperii*—the formal definition of imperial power in Rome.

In 69, in the Lex de Imperio de Vespasiani—the document granting total imperial power to Emperor Vespasian—there was a certain Clause VI that basically could have been written by your very own Justice Department. According to historian Anthony A. Barrett, Clause VI gave the *princeps* "the right and power . . . to do what he thinks to be to the advantage of the state, thus technically giving him the discretion to violate even existing laws."

In short, monarchy on a stick, courtesy of the senate, the very instrument by which things were supposed to be prevented from becoming a monarchy.

Ring a bell?

Say what you will about how much you'd like to see George W. Bush and Dick Cheney kicked to death by nine-year-old girls: their pet legal team did a marvelous job of pimping powers specifically denied to the president by the Constitution. Most notable of these were the skeevy thug-boy legal manipulations of Dick Cheney's legal team, headed by the brilliantly diabolical David Addington, Cheney's legal adviser, and John Yoo, the assistant to the attorney general (and ex-clerk to salt-pillar-of-misanthropy Supreme Court Justice Clarence Thomas). Yoo really took shameless, yes-man buttock-suckling to soaring new heights in terms of selling the great American experiment down the river to sate his quest for personal advancement and mastery of *nihil abnuentum, dum dominationis aspiceretur*.

Yoo, the Pablo Picasso of constitutional law, went

to town deconstructing the Constitution and sticking it back together again in wild new postmodern ways that really pleased the big dogs by handing them the exciting, creative, barely legal justifications they craved in order to ignore the Foreign Intelligence Surveillance Act, the Geneva Convention, and the U.N. Convention Against Torture. Once justified, they were able to freely wiretap everybody, beat the pecan pie out of "enemy combatants" up to the point of organ rupture and otherwise heel-kick oilcans up the collective international hinterlands with extreme prejudice and no fear of retribution.

Besides being a contributor to the Patriot Act and a coauthor on the now famous "torture memo," Yoo made his greatest legal contribution—the *Guernica* of his law spin-art codex, as it were—in that wacky piece of doctrine called the Unitary Executive Theory, a veritable Olympic triple-toe-loop of balls-to-the-wall legal hyper-audacity.

This theory, sometimes called the "Yoo Doctrine," argues that an incredibly garbled, far-out, and über-Federalist interpretation of some unrelated stuff in the Constitution creates a "hierarchical, unified executive department under the direct control of the President" and "asserts that all executive power must be in the President's hands, without exception."

I like to call it the "John Yoo Theory of the Executive 'Because I Said So' Dick-Slap." It's everything a Dictator for Life needs in terms of the right legal all-in-one tool for the job. If you wanna be a *princeps legibus solutus*—a princeps not bound by the laws—it helps if everyone else around you with any kind of executive power gets really confused by some overt proclamation of the legality of what you're doing and therefore does nothing but stand around haplessly with their thumbs up their eunuchs.

Anyway, Yoo's legal witchcraft has been mind-bendingly useful for drop-kicking America over the cliff into executive totalitarianism. It's basically the judicial form of the *Ring of the Nibelungen*.

Although nothing in the Constitution actually allows this, President George W. Bush, using these extra-turbo powers, signed a howling maelstrom of executive orders and bastardized hundreds of law provisions with his own decorative signing statements, despite the fact that the Supreme Court specifically banned such line-item vetos.

Plus, as I mentioned earlier, President Bush also ushered in a historic amount of National Security Presidential Directives (NSPDs) and Homeland Security Presidential Directives (HSPDs)—little extra-judicial, extra-presidential snacky-treats that are "extra legal" but still have the full "force and effect" of law.

For example, there are executive orders that our executive ordered so he could entrust himself with absolute power in case of a "catastrophic emergency" (defined as "any incident, regardless of location, that results in extraordinary levels of mass casualties, damage, or disruption severely affecting the U.S. population, infrastructure, environment, economy, or government function")—thus overriding and jettisoning the entire federal branch of government, which might force him to exercise undue restraint, caution or jurisprudence.

Booyah.

Anyway, like I was saying, if possible, when becoming emperor, always follow a real dog of a warm-up act. Classically, at the beginning of a regime change, it is usually a good idea and trustworthy gesture for the new leader to renounce the evildoings of the old administration and establish as much distance from the outgoing disgrace as possible.

When I assumed power in Rome, I naturally acted really disgusted by Tiberius and renounced all his old banishments and legal cases he'd built against his enemies. Your new American president is obviously going to have to make a show of loudly denouncing everything the Bush administration did from the minute they stole the office, and exterminate all the old loyal slaves.

Which invites certain questions:

Q: Since two thirds of these HSPDs and NSPDs are classified and are going to be classified indefinitely (and there are dozens of them and they are filled with draconian erosions of your civil liberties and wild proclamations of executive privilege), and since, technically speaking, if these executive orders, directives, memoranda, etc., were documents that originated in the executive branch (i.e., they were not passed as statute or handed down as a decision from a court), they will stay in force until they are rescinded, overruled or superseded by another president. (But you still wouldn't know what they were, because they're classified and declassifying anything is usually too much of a time-consuming pain in the ass for a busy president to be bothered with.)

However.

Even if the White House records never see the light of day because all the e-mail hard drives were destroyed, every decision of the Bush administration that actually got turned into policy will have left a snail-trail of documents in one or more of the agencies. If I, as your next president, felt like it, I could disclose this iridescent slime of paper trails.

All these massive executive-power-consolidating, pound-you-up-the-fanny-whenever-the-urge-so-takes-me directives *could* simply be ordered not to exist anymore by me, as your next president, with the simple stroke of my pen.

So, what then will I, as your next president, do to undo these horrible, frightening and top-secret presidential directives that would dangerously give me a substantial legal platform upon which to tyrannize and enslave you, unchecked by anything but my own sense of discretion?

A: Nothing.

I'm just not going to talk about them—then you will forget about them and it will be as if they never existed.

They're not important.

(Although privately it does give me a chuckle to know that there's a whole lot of cold war documents that you still don't get to read either.)

But, as a consolation prize, I bet Britney Spears will

make another comeback! And boy will you hate it. It will be the only thing you talk about for months.

Q: Since these presidential directives are classified, are you, as citizens, subject to prosecution under law-esque things you're not allowed to read?

A: I was curious about this, so I asked one of my national security law experts. He said that, generally speaking, executive orders are not enforceable against citizens the way that civil or criminal laws are . . . because they're not actually "laws."

However!

The Military Commissions order of November 13, 2001—in which President Bush established military tribunals to try non-U.S. citizens who were suspected of ties to al-Qaeda—has matured and ripened into the Military Commissions system now underway at Guantánamo Bay. The order was overturned by the Supreme Court, but reinstated by Congress through the Military Commissions Act. So *the military commissions now have a basis in statute*, not just executive order.

Meaning!

You should bear in mind that while these things aren't technically *law*-laws yet, you *can* most likely be prosecuted under any order or directive or napkin with ballpoint scribbles on it that I happen to get a statute for. You think it's hard getting a statute? I can get a statute practically at the speed of *thought*. I blow my nose and statutes come out. The presidential directives this joker phoned in are just my beachhead. PDs and signing statements is about to get *crazy*, yo.

Say someone were to ask me, "Oh, Holy Presidential Emperor Gaius Caligula, will you personally and unilaterally issue an executive order on Day 1 that overrules all the Bush administration's memoranda on torture, hubristic executive privilege, the wholesale looting of the third world and neo-slavery, and thereby restore sanity, equilibrium and the rule of law to American society?"

I would say, "No! But you'll be glad later that I didn't."

I can't tell you why, though, because it's a secret. You'll just have to trust me.

I can only tell you that signing statements are going to get whomped all over documents like restroom graffiti whenever I feel like anything could impair my death grip on foreign relations or national security, or somehow otherwise limit the wildest power-grabby ejaculations of my executive dream team.

Hey, historically speaking, you want a strong man in charge now that your middle class is eroded back to non-English-speaking busboy levels of poverty. You're angry and you feel betrayed.

So let's haul our collective jackboots back out of the basement, pull ourselves up by their little black straps, wrap ourselves in Old Glory, blame Islam and stomp some third-world oil-country ass!

That's what sitting on the throne and being a fully fledged Dictato-Fascisto-Klepto-Imperio-Hoolicrat is all about: rocking all night with the tangy taste of old-fashioned, unchecked sovereign authority!

Since the beginning of history, really important people have been having top-secret meetings to which you have never, ever been invited, and these meetings dictate the course of your lives. Until you worm your terrible way through some quirk of destiny into one of those rooms, my dears, you're just going to have to *relax.*

Within a short time of assuming the throne in Rome, I got the senate to grant me some ever-more-fantastic new titles: Pontifex Maximus, high priest of all gods and chief interpreter of sacred law, and also Castrorum Filius (son of the armies), Pater Exercituum (father of the armies—dig how I was *both*), and my personal favorite, Optimus Maximus Caesar.

Just in case anyone was confused as to how heavy a Caesar I was.

I realized that, as emperor, I would unfortunately have to become inured to doing a lot of killing, so I rolled up my sleeves and started with Gemellus.

Gemellus was a horrid fat boy, always coughing. I was told he was taking an antidote for poison with his cough medicine, which meant he was obviously engaging—or soon to engage—in a conspiracy against me, because he obviously suspected I was poisoning him.

This was all the more insulting since he had only recently been made my adopted son. The *ingratitude.* I allowed him to kill himself, but I should have sealed him into a toolshed full of cobras.

I will put this same ruthlessness to work for you.

I pledge to do what must be done to get everyone before they get you, America. Free country or no free country, democracy or no democracy—at the end of the day, say what you want . . .

You have to admit this: you're *American*. Naked displays of raw proactive bully-power put a tingling feeling in your undershorts. You like to see the bad guys get it.

Might dictates victory, victory dictates history, and dictators dictate laws, which confer power, which confer might, which kicks ass. So, don't mess with Daddy, or I'll get my butter knife and cut your head back to the fat meat.

Right? You love it.

MY FIRST HUNDRED DAYS AS YOUR PRESIDENTIAL MESSIAH

Right after I down my celebratory Big Gulp cup of hummingbird tongues and enjoy the sight of the current cabinet begging for their lives, I am going to repair some things that have been nagging at me.

1. I will make a point of following Australia's moral lead and apologize to the Native Americans for the genocide upon which this nation was founded. The Native American shall once again be the proud symbol of America. What, after all, does that kind of apology cost?

It's an excellent PR psyop mindfuck to suddenly become a concerned champion of something you were directly responsible for destroying. These days, if you go to the Exxon or Shell Web sites without knowing whose they were, you'd think they were the Sierra Club's for all the wood ducks and pine-sucking vegans.

2. I am claiming *droit du seigneur* and retroactive *primae noctis* on the brides of all my employees. A leader should always be given the privilege of sleeping with your wife before you do.

Maidenheads have been the domain of the powerful since the epic of Gilgamesh. You can't say the Mesopotamians never gave us anything useful. (Well, you can, but I can't. I have too many employees. Wink wink nudge nudge.)

3. Here's a surprising little statistic: Despite the fact that most Americans think the Union Jack is something bachelorette parties can order as a special service at a male strip club (and for that matter, most Americans think Chippendale was originally a male strip club), 18 percent of Americans actually own a passport.

When I claim my divine right as your Holy American Emperor, there will never be a need for you to travel overseas again. Should wily citizens succeed in escaping the United States, they will be guaranteed to find a Hooters in every country. My reach as a corporate brand is infinite. Dissidents will soon realize that all efforts to escape the Holy Imperial United States are futile and unnecessary since they will be so happy and perfectly fulfilled here.

4. As your first official cock-rock president, I will retire the stodgy Dad-vehicle that is Air Force One.

Sure, there are nice things to be said about the flying Edsel parked over there at Andrews Air Force Base in Hangar 19. It's an OK way to travel, particularly when you're accompanied by the Secret Service, enough firepower, communications and surveillance equipment for a small army, a complete motorcade full of bulletproof limousines, an extremely well-stocked pharmacy and, best of all, what we presidents like to refer to as "the Football"—a sealed leather "doomsday briefcase" containing all the codes necessary to launch a nuclear strike, carried by a seasoned career military "ball carrier" with a cool name like "Lieutenant Commander Pat DeQuattro."

I mean, yes, it is "the ultimate power trip." It has shielding that blocks the effects of a nuclear blast.

But the thing is a whole fucking city block long and s-s-s-slow.

So, as your president and earthly representative, I will consider it my duty to update my look by taking the Football and flying around in a pimped-out Raptor F-22 with customized, dirt-modified diamond-tuck zebra-fur NASCAR seats, an absinthe wet bar and a four-direction PVC sex-harness. Needless to say, I will also require the constant medical ministrations of my "nurse" Ayesha, who will gun me full of opiates, and a standing and ready team of Blue Angel stunt pilots to drive me around and go into occasional controlled tailspins and barrel rolls to keep me entertained.

This way, if I decide that I want to phone in some nuclear launch codes, we can just blast over there ourselves and drop the fucker *immediately*. At the speed of decision.

That's how I roll. You, however, are hereby condemned to fly coach on American Airlines.

(I'm sorry, I just blew ambrosia out my nose, I was laughing so hard.)

Also, I intend to require all federal airfields to begin construction on their new federal airfield casinos. There's nothing more mind-meltingly boring, hideous and revenue-sucking than a federal airfield, except maybe the Federal Helium Reserve we keep in Amarillo, Texas, at the Bush Dome reservoir just in case our nation ever needs a fleet of combat dirigibles.

5. The presidential image will also be revamped, in order to reflect the modern totalitarian flair of the twenty-first century.

There's more to decorating for tyranny than just living in an enormous pink marble penthouse filled with brass planters, leopard pelts, stolen museum objects, human skulls, 18k gold-plated Kalashnikovs, and Matterhorn-size mounds of blow.

It's the damnedest thing, but I swear, the minute you are suddenly given an empire and/or fame and billions of dollars, you are seized by a Michael Jackson–cum-Scarface-like need to create a personal petting zoo of endangered species. It comes with the territory.

Nebuchadnezzar, for example, used to ride around on a lion with a snake around its neck. Nero was accused of setting the fire in A.D. 64 that hit Rome just to clear fifty acres of space to build his own Neverland Ranch and personal zoo.

Paris Hilton had a pet kinkajou until it went for her eyes in a lingerie shop. John Quincy Adams kept an alligator, swam nude in the Potomac and liked having sex outdoors.

Saddam Hussein's eldest son, Uday, had lions, a bear, a cheetah and Internet pictures Photoshopped to look like the naked Bush twins on his walls.

William Randolph Hearst introduced the moronic llama into the United States. Teddy Roosevelt kept a bear and a lion as pets at the White House. Philip II of Spain enjoyed collecting dwarves.

As your Holy Royal President, I vow to bring Lou Dobbs to the White House as a reward for services rendered, put him up in the Lincoln Bedroom, then fill a polar bear with Adderall and throw it in with him at around three A.M., while blasting Slayer's *Reign in Blood*.

And then I'm putting the footage on YouTube.

Entertainment!

It is the mandate of heaven.

7

THE ECONOMY: READY TO LOOT WITH THE BIG DOGS

Pecunia non olet.
(Money has no smell.)
—Emperor Vespasian

Imperialism is the monopoly stage of capitalism.
—Lenin

The comfort of the rich depends on an abundance of the poor.
—Voltaire

Under the gold standard, a free banking system stands as the protector of an economy's stability and balanced growth . . . Government bonds are not backed by tangible wealth, only by the government's promise to pay out of future tax revenues . . . The abandonment of the gold standard made it possible for the welfare statists to use the banking system as a means to an unlimited expansion of credit . . .

> But the fact is that there are now more claims outstanding than real assets . . . In the absence of the gold standard, there is no way to protect savings from confiscation through inflation. There is no safe store of value . . . **Deficit spending is simply a scheme for the confiscation of wealth** [emphasis mine]."
>
> **—Alan Greenspan**

Wondering what to buy the Machiavellian autocrat in your life who has everything?

The top floor of Bergdorf Goodman carries an 18k gold replica of a human skull, for $3,495. I like those.

When things were getting rough on the poor back in Rome, I would hold a *congiarium*—assemble a huge amount of gold and silver coins—and literally pour them from the roof of the palace for about a week. Crowds would come in droves and trample each other trying to get a piece of the action. So as incentive for the mob to remain orderly, I also made sure that big chunks of iron were also hurled down with the money. Some of the greedier eunuchs were killed or injured, but this way, more people got a turn.

President Bush, to revivify your tanking economy, distributed a largesse in 2008 of up to $600 in tax rebates per person; ironically, it was not unlike the largesse he distributed at the beginning of his presidency, when everyone got a $300 tax rebate because the nation had a surplus, and the president couldn't figure out how to spend all that money on roads or bridges or infrastructure, so he gave it all back so you could buy iPods.

The anvils being thrown down from the palace roof with the Bush golden shower consist of the fact that the $600 per head is essentially a high-interest shark-loan coming from the global economic equivalent of E-ZPaycheckAdvance.com. This deficit spending is borrowed against your future income taxes, taken out of future income from the jobs you just lost. In short, you are eating your children in the form of their education and/or all their hope of advancement past the blue collar.

The repo men are coming for America. We may have to sell Louisiana back to the French. Nanny states like Puerto Rico may have to be put in foster countries. Debtor's prisons? Hmm! Could be.

It is time to ask yourselves, *Qui bono?* Who benefits? Who benefits when America can't afford to buy its own onion rings anymore?

History is full of clever opportunists. One of Rome's more entrepreneurial sorts was a guy called Crassus, who assembled his own fire department from a team of slaves. If your house caught fire, he'd offer to buy it from you for a fraction of its value. If you agreed to sell it to him, he'd put the fire out. If you didn't sell, he'd watch it burn down and heckle you about what an idiot you were for not selling it to him.

The larger workings of the American economy are really very similar.

If you have to ask, "Hey, did we just have a big economic-blackout decade and wake up in the gutter with our pants around our ankles, and did someone actually scorch the Coors logo into our backs with a homemade branding iron?"—well, the answer is yes. Wealth has successfully been concentrated back to 1929 levels of inequality. In the words of the frat boys from *Animal House*: "Hey! You fucked up! You trusted us!"

The myth behind the American brand of democracy is built on the touching punch line that "all men are created equal."

Let's put it this way: Speaking for myself, as a member of the ruling elite, I had more property than you do when I was about four months old. I was allowed to torture my own servants when I was about nine, with more or less total impunity. (This, again, is not abnormal ruling-class behavior. Don Carlos of Spain used to do the same thing when he was a boy—plus, he tortured horses and once bit the head off a ring snake.)

I think we can safely revise this sentiment to "all men are not quite created equal." I mean, let's face it: You aren't even allowed to access the online version of *Departures* magazine without entering the last four digits of a platinum AmEx card. You need a biometric thumbprint device just to access a Bloomberg subscription. You don't even get to *read* about the truly rich.

Why?

Well, we have stuff so radically fabulous and hyper-expensive that *you're not even allowed to know it exists*. If you had any sophisticated idea of the painfully sharp contrast between the way superelites in your country live compared with the way you live, your brain would pop like a coconut under the Panzer-tread of outrageous fortune and you'd never be happy again. Your life of quiet desperation would become one of shrill and piercing desperation.

Think of Haiti, at the end of the Papa Doc Duvalier regime. There was a rumor that nuns who had been working with the poor were allowed to tour the mansion for the first time after the family was ousted, and several of them vomited because of the outrageous dichotomy between the lives they'd been living, down with the Squalidictorians, and the life the president was living. The sudden ascent into nosebleed levels of opulence gave the nuns the *bends*.

Nowadays, if You People saw how we lived, it would be even worse.

You'd overturn police cars and burn down your own neighborhoods again and again and never be satisfied until every last gold-sandaled, oyster-sucking, hyperelite peckerwood fop like me ended up with his head in a KFC bucket.

According to Nobel laureate Joseph Stiglitz, 5.3 million more Americans are living in poverty now than at the beginning of the Bush presidency: "America's class structure may not have arrived there yet, but it's heading in the direction of Brazil's and Mexico's."

Hey, remember just a few years back when we had a surplus and the dollar was worth something?

Special pains were taken at the highest levels to fuck that up.

Think of it as economic drunkorexia: You People needed to get starved of vital nutrients so that the upper 1 percent could have ice sculptures of David Beckham that urinate vodka.

Just as Chinese cat food is now inalterably associated with dead cats in the American consciousness, the Enron-ification of America has resulted in a tanking of trust in the American brand around the world.

Brands are built on trust. America's economy, however, since the erosion of the gold standard, has been built on credit: *credit that was extended to America based on trust in the strength, endurance and credibility of the American brand*—a trust that has now been severely gang-banged by the very leaders in whom you placed your public trust.

That's not because you're idiots. It's because you're hapless peons.

"We are now saddled with a rigged economy based on record-setting trade and fiscal deficits," said Dr. Chalmers Johnson.

Marshall Auerback, an international financial strategist, says we have become a "Blanche Dubois economy" heavily dependent on "the kindness of strangers."

Well, if you've read Tennessee Williams, you know that everyone eventually gets wise to the fact that Blanche is a bipolar nymphomaniac and blackout drunk. Then she is publicly humiliated, raped by her sister's husband, has a nervous breakdown and eventually has to be committed to a sanitarium.

Q: How did we get into this monstrous state of affairs?
A: Monstrous affairs of state!

Here's a shocker: Your government hasn't been telling you how screwed up your economy really is, because they're not done raping it yet.

Right now, the economy is a whole lot like a fairly good-looking brain-dead chick in a persistent vegetative coma. You can't really wake her up, but there's things she's still good for.

To bastardize journalist Kevin Phillips: Officially speaking, you've been lied to for years about what's in the collective checking account.

Your official statistics are anything but an accurate portrayal of how dismal the economy really is. Numbers for the consumer price index (CPI), unemployment rates and the gross domestic product (GDP)—basically, the three main indicators of the health of the economy—have all been hopelessly perverted by fact-erosion since the Kennedy administration, as each subsequent administration opts to shave off ugly statistics in order to paint a rosier picture of your future. The result? A truth gap that has grown progressively more Grand Canyonlike over the years, in thrall to a tendency that economic analyst John Williams nicknamed the "Pollyanna Creep."

Each administration decided that certain indicators brought the economic mood too far down—so they gradually stopped factoring all the bummers into the number pile. Nixon, for example, decided not to include figures for the volatile food and energy markets in "core" inflation figures, resulting in a figure that economic commentator Barry Ritholtz called "inflation *ex*-inflation"—in other words, inflation figures with all the nasty inflation-y bits taken out.

According to Kevin Phillips in *Harpers*, the Reagan administration further bunged-up the CPI figure by diddling the housing market numbers, using, instead of the actual figure, a figure "based on what a homeowner might get for renting his or her house" (leaving out the question of where said homeowner might live, with his or her house rented out like that).

Why keep this picture so artificially bright?

"Who profits from a low-growth U.S. economy hidden under statistical camouflage[?] Might it be Washington politicos and affluent elites, anxious to mislead voters, coddle the financial markets, and tamp down expensive cost-of-living increases for wages and pensions?" asks Phillips.

Dearie me: *Might it?*

First things first: When I am your Divine President, the first economic bummer I am going to erase is Kevin Phillips.

Here's your truthy dose of tough love: Your actual unemployment rate is somewhere between 9 and 12 percent, minimum. Your actual inflation rate is more like 7 to 10 percent, and probably more like in the serious double digits. Your interest rates are likely to go up as a hedge against inflation. Uh oh.

So, I'd say we all need to turn to our new state religious system for hope and guidance.

Let's call it our faith-based economy.

It's the exact method that made Enron great: Its stock prices were always based on its future projections, which were entirely fictional . . . but very hopeful and optimistic.

It survived just like Tinkerbell, as long as everyone

clapped their hands, thought beautiful thoughts and *believed* in it.

Enron just didn't have the rude will and raw bully-power it takes to keep riding the imaginary wave.

But, as long as you are technically still between the window you jumped out of and the sidewalk below . . . you're flying like Superman!

In terms of the American economy, sometimes you have to take coma girl's arms and wave them around a little so it looks like she's doing the hula.

It's about hope.

It's not fraud if everyone believes in it. It's more like Santa Claus.

Ask yourself: Is there a Santa Claus?

Thousands of tiny faces with big moist eyes want you to say yes. If you don't, then you're a very small, heartless person, who hates children and America.

The great thing about me is, I really don't choose favorites, particularly when it comes to inevitables like death and taxes. I am merely a tireless arm enforcing the will of a vengeful and jealous god.

You think the middle class has taken a beating recently? Of course they have!

We're getting a fresh start, America: I intend to make sure *everyone* takes a beating. But *especially* the very rich.

No more sneaky back-alley cash smuggling. No Swiss banks, offshore accounts or empty offices in the Cayman Islands. I am going to appoint an entire intelligence wing devoted to forensic asset location, and I will personally scrutinize the records pertaining to all the financial credit records of any private citizens I suspect to be extremely wealthy.

Back in Rome, I arranged murders just so I could seize the personal properties of my more affluent friends. Now *that's* a level playing field. After what the elites have done to your country in the last seven years? You should *want* to see them sweat-lodged into jerky.

We don't have ghastly enough punishments in place to scare straight an entrenched culture of corruption and keep Harvard MBAs from looting America's dumber and less fortunate, but I am going to change all that. If you really want disincentives for this kind of thing, you really, *really* need to condemn said MBAs to public executions and compulsory mock battles.

Barbaric, you say? Be honest: Who doesn't want to see opposing corporate law firms go after each other with electric turkey knives at Yankee Stadium?

Besides, this form of justice pays for itself in live ticket sales and TV contracts.

Let me tell you a little story about your very own lives.

Once, a long, long time ago—six years—soo-o-o-o long ago that nobody even remembers, there was a boy named Thomas Cruikshank. In the 1960s, Tommy was the vice president of an oil-field services company called Halliburton.

When Mr. Cruikshank was finally so rich he couldn't carry any more money, he stepped down and handed his golden Halliburton pope hat to his good friend Mr. Dick Cheney.

Mr. Cheney went on, in the year 2000, to become

Vice President of the Entire World, with Dominion over All Powers and Energies both Temporal and Thermonuclear.

In early 2001, President Bush's top foreign policy priority was to address the nation's "energy crisis" by increasing the flow of petroleum from suppliers abroad to U.S. markets (because he came from a family whose dynastic wealth is still very much involved with the black gold).

Mr. Bush told his friend Mr. Cheney to create an Energy Task Force, which would help dictate energy policy throughout the land. Cheney and his buddy Ken Lay, Emperor of Enron, had secret meetings with all the High Pontiffs of Energy from all over the world: Exxon Mobil Corporation, Conoco, Shell Oil Company, BP America Inc., Chevron and others. "Virtually every major oil and diversified energy company," said the *New York Times*.

Names of the participants are still a secret (classified—PSYCH!) but non-mainstream journalists claim that former Energy Department officials said all the most important white men were there: Karl Rove, Andy Card, Energy secretary Spencer Abraham and perhaps even Dick Cheney's old bosom pal, Mr. Cruikshank, who was then on the board of directors of Williams Companies (a *Fortune* 500 company specializing in natural gas exploration, production and processing, with numerous assets in petroleum and electricity generation). Another guest was Curt Hebert, chairman of the Federal Energy Regulatory Commission (FERC).

(Environmental groups, however, weren't really invited. They hadn't made major contributions to Republican candidates like everyone else. At night, instead of resting on pillow-top beds at the Hay-Adams, they were forced to sleep on paper napkins in the parking garage.)

According to documents obtained through the Freedom of Information Act, the happy bunch of good friends used this month of meetings to pore over detailed maps of Iraqi oil fields, pipelines and refineries and to give detailed energy policy recommendations.

They wanted to establish new sources for oil and ensure uninterrupted access to the oil reserves owned by the icky brown Arab men who once tried to kill the president's own father—without whom the president would be a staggering wino with his pants around his ankles, a tattoo of Yosemite Sam, and a crumpled Dunkin' Donuts cup full of pennies, stumbling around a Texas reservoir, eating garbage and using his dog as a towel.

Mr. Cheney was a very powerful warlock. His sorcery enabled him to orchestrate U.S. energy policies in a way that would *magically and perfectly anticipate U.S. military strategy.*

Amazingly enough, the documents from these meetings—full of plans to occupy Iraq and take their oil—were dated March 2001 . . . a full *six months* before the attacks of 9/11, proving that Mr. Cheney was *psychic* about Saddam Hussein's connection to 9/11.

The bitter environmentalists—still angry at not having been invited to the meetings—suggested that America's suddenly very aggressive foreign policy was being driven by the personal interests of the president and the vice president and their powerful friends, who all stood to gain handsomely from such a turn of events.

Poor bark-eating, egret-diddling hippies.

One thing the Energy Popes did do, however, was discuss deregulating the nation's electricity sector, because it was another way in which they could all become even more whoppingly prosperous.

According to a November 2002 article by David Lazarus for the *San Francisco Chronicle* online,

> We know, thanks to documents just released by federal regulators, that energy providers Williams and AES conspired to drive electricity prices higher during the worst of the California power crisis.
>
> What most people don't know, though, is that board members of both companies have links to the White House, as do directors of other energy heavyweights that have received subpoenas . . .
>
> There's no evidence of any wrongdoing on the part of these board members. But their ties to the first and second Bush administrations once again raise troubling questions about what federal authorities knew about the energy crisis and when they knew it . . .
>
> Take the case of Thomas Cruikshank, who has served on the Williams board for the past 12 years. He also happens to be the retired chief executive officer of Halliburton and personally selected Vice President Dick Cheney to succeed him at [Halliburton] . . .

Did Cheney contact his corporate mentor to discuss the situation in California? Did Cruikshank ever mention that Williams was profiting handsomely from the state's troubles (it made an extra $10 million in just two weeks)?

Who knows? The White House is keeping details of Cheney's energy-policy talks to itself . . .

Meddling goblins from FERC were *investigating* Williams Companies (and another company called the AES Corporation) on suspicion both companies had manufactured a fake power shortage in California for two weeks in April and May of 2000 by shutting down a power plant, so that Williams Companies could charge turbo-inflated premium rates per megawatt hour to provide "emergency" power for California's grid—at roughly a 400 percent markup on the actual price.

The FERC goblins had "incriminating audio tapes" of a Williams official and an AES power plant operator talking about keeping a Southern California power plant off-line. Mr. Cheney knew this information could be very bad for the whole project of energy deregulation—particularly since California's governor, Gray Davis, was starting to smell a rat.

But—behold—a holy testimony to the awesome power of absolute executive power.

Mr. Cheney used his incredible warlock skills to issue a direct executive order to seal the FERC documents. And they're still sealed to this day! FERC entered into confidential settlements with Williams and other companies, which forfeited monies "owed" to them by California for the costly "emergency" power. But they didn't have to tell California officials anything about their skeevy market manipulations or confess any collusion or wrongdoing, and now everything's fine.

Just to keep things extra-safe, Cheney and pal Karl Rove organized a smear campaign. On May 21, 2001—five days after unveiling his new official energy policy—Cheney told Tim Russert on *Meet the Press* that all the energy problems in California were Governor Gray Davis's fault.

Shortly thereafter, poor Gray Davis was booted out of his governorship midseason and replaced by a big Austrian Republican movie star.

And the moral of the story is, What's a moral?

Hahahaha. Boom.

No, actually, the moral is this: Nobody thinks about this major crime committed against the people of California anymore, because so many other crimes have been committed since then that nobody really remembers that one anymore.

Hey, energy policy fixing, collusion and insider hazing weren't the only bandits that hit town during the last decade. Those were just the woodwinds and the tympani of the entire orchestra of madcap economic tomfoolery that handed America its own fiscal ass.

Next came the big Vegas horn section—in the form of the amazing inflatable mortgage.

Here's another little story.

Once upon a time, before his 2006 appointment to

the office of secretary of the Treasury, Hank Paulson was chairman and CEO of Goldman Sachs.

Goldman Sachs is a freakishly smart and extremely naughty global investment bank. Its strategy is to bet on certain things to fail, and then *help* them fail by taking a "short position" and playing both sides of the investment fence. It's a wonderful technique that creates a win-win for Goldman Sachs, and a lose-lose for anyone who happens to not be Goldman Sachs.

Actor-economist Ben Stein wagged his fingers and reprimanded Goldman Sachs in the *New York Times* for cashing in on the subprime mortgage crisis, because Goldman Sachs knew very well that the mortgages were diseased meat.

Sayeth Stein, in economy-speak: "As Goldman was peddling C.M.O.'s . . . it was also shorting the junk on a titanic scale through index sales—showing, at least to me, how horrible a product it believed it was selling."

CMOs are "collateralized mortgage obligations." Or, in other words, CMOs are pools of sickly subprime mortgages, created to be "special purpose entities," i.e., *completely separate* from the institutions—like Goldman Sachs—that made them.

Bonds were then issued by these special, separate, *nothing-to-do-with-Goldman-Sachs-really* CMO entities to you, the lucky investor.

"It is bad enough to have been selling this stuff," grumbled Mr. Stein. "It is far worse when the sellers were, in effect, simultaneously shorting the stuff they were selling, or making similar bets . . . If a top economist at Goldman Sachs was saying housing was in trouble, why did Goldman continue to underwrite junk mortgage issues into the market?"

That's a tough one. Um . . . altruism? Humanitarianism? The greater public good? A fair and balanced perspective?

This hustle toward aggressively privatizing absolutely everything is the most fun I've had since I put a brothel in the Imperial Palace and made various senators' wives work the "mule room."

I'm having my Hummer custom painted Burberry plaid. You?

You think that's skeevy? Dig this: Investment banks have been bidding up oil prices in order to make a profit from you, the consumer. Oh! Shockers.

My own evil dwarves in the brokerage industry call it "painting the tape." It's not only unethical; it is also illegal to do this with any commodity, let alone a vital resource like oil—but never mind.

"Painting the tape," defined by InvestorWords.com:

> The illegal practice in which traders buy and sell a specific security among themselves, creating the illusion of high trading volume and significant investor interest, which can attract unsuspecting investors who might then buy the stock and enable the traders to profit.

Which leads us to "Oil Price Gouging: From Enron with Love," by David R. Usher:

> Savvy investment firms and avaricious lawyers analyzed the Enron case—realizing they could turn a

> huge buck on oil futures—*so long as they tacitly let oil companies constrain the oil supply without manipulating the supply directly themselves* [emphasis mine] . . . Enron took advantage of deregulation in California, manipulating electricity prices by raiding the futures market, overscheduling power lines, and creating fears about shortages.

Not only that, but the deregulation in California enabled the boys in the energy trading business to come up with cool names for their market manipulation strategies such as "Fat Boy," "Death Star," "Black Widow," "Big Foot," "Red Congo" and "Get Shorty."

In 2006, a couple of months after Hank Paulson left Goldman Sachs to become secretary of the Treasury, and just before the November elections, Goldman Sachs made gasoline prices fall by suddenly selling off six billion dollars in gasoline futures contracts.

On LewRockwell.com, Peter Stojan wrote:

> This type of aggressive selling will result in selling by others who will receive margin calls they can't meet. And by trend followers, who will suddenly dump gasoline and other commodities . . .
>
> . . . Goldman doesn't lose money . . . the actual money put up comes from institutions, hedge funds and other unlucky saps that trusted Goldman to manage the commodity index as a hedge against inflation—not to bail out of $6 billion in contracts over a few weeks. The result: Unlucky saps—Major

losses. Goldman—Zero losses and their man running the Treasury. Which side of this trade would you want to be on?

Incredibly, every time a Bush is in office, a sudden coincidental black plague of unlucky junk bondage enslaves the mass populace of the nation, while a few of their friends become spankdankerously wealthy and don't have to pay taxes anymore. Remember all of the savings and loan, real estate and junk bond scandals that took place between 1989 and 1992, when George H. W. Bush was president?

Total coincidence.

Let's borrow two timely quotes from the bestseller *Rich Dad, Poor Dad*, by Robert Kiyosaki and Sharon Lechter.

1. "Financial intelligence is a synergy of accounting, investing, marketing and law. Combine those four technical skills and making money with money is easier."

And,

2. "Remember the Golden Rule. He who has the gold makes the rules."

Synergy! Work with your friends—print your own money.

Deregulate and privatize federal markets with little or no oversight, and make the rules hugely obscure and largely inscrutable even to the priest class of corporate lawyers who wrote them.

Then, use more lawyers to find crazy loopholes and pioneer rambunctious new arbitrage opportunities—

i.e., figure out what shell game isn't *specifically illegal yet*, and use these little nude patches of nonlegislation to shake little old ladies upside down by their collapsed ankles and make abnormal profits.

Then, use this booty to grease lawmakers and influence policy, and you can eat your sashimi off any groin in the free world.

Rolling blackouts! Fictional Nigerian power barges! Utilities up 400 percent!

Round and round and round she goes—it's whiplash agony and ecstasy. America's going native: The whole economic landscape is being turned into one big Indian casino. Big payoffs, big losses.

But hey, you gotta admit, these aren't your grandpa's stodgy old utilities! These babies are wearing motorcycle jackets and smokin'.

Here's another great thing I'm going to do for the American economy. Most American presidents have to choose whether their priority is to invest in "guns" (read: increased military spending) or "butter" (read: handouts to the morally inferior).

I am going to do all previous presidents one better and give America guns AND butter *at the same time*. I am going to give every single American their very own loaded Colt 1991A automatic government pistol . . . covered with rich, delicious, creamery butter.

I figure that this way, half of you will accidentally eliminate yourselves and/or each other within about four days. This will help bring affordable health care much more into reach for those of you smart enough not to touch the guns.

* * *

In 1990, Donald Trump was two billion dollars in bank debt he had no intention of repaying ("Donald Trump had become the Brazil of Manhattan," wrote biographer Gwenda Blair).

Trump was completely tanking, but he was in so deep with various financial and lending institutions who had fallen all over themselves to buy into the fame-power and credibility of the Trump name that they bailed him out for two reasons:

1. They were so embarrassed they fell for it, and

2. They would have been wiped out if they let him default.

According to Ms. Blair, Trump revealed his powerful secret to conquering financial adversity once, in a meeting to promote another one of his signature, view-eating housing developments: "You know," he said, "what New York really needs—besides this project—is to reduce its debt. And let me tell you—this is something I know—it's easy! You just don't pay!"

America is in the process of heeding this sage advice. I like to call it "Pull-My-Finger Economics."

Remember when the dollar was actually worth something? Chop! Socky!

Remember when the Chinese pulled the Oriental rug out from under our currency at the end of 2007? Chinese officials signaled their plans to diversify their $1.43 trillion of foreign exchange reserves, and fried our collective wontons.

WHAMMO. It was the economic equivalent of

that scene in the Bruce Lee movie *Game of Death* where nobody can believe that a small, wiry Asian man fan-kicks the pie out of Kareem Abdul-Jabbar.

According to *Bloomberg*: "The dollar fell against all 16 of the most-active currencies, declining to the weakest versus the Canadian dollar since the end of a fixed exchange rate in 1950." All because China said it was going to "diversify out of dollar holdings."

And, curiously, that's *exactly* what Dick Cheney did in 2006, when he put between ten and twenty-five million dollars of his personal assets into the American Century International Bond, a fund whose "prospectus limits dollar exposure to 25% of assets" and has "only 6% of assets in dollars."

This may strike you as an ever so slightly unpatriotic thing for the vice president of your nation to do.

Maybe just a little nihilistic.

Kinda-sorta like speeding through all the red lights in Capitol Hill in a hospital zone, blasting Wagner's *Götterdämmerung* out the gull-wing doors of your Krupp Panzer IV, while wearing a Sudanese blood-diamond tiara, eating a Cuban sandwich and ripping bootleg DVDs *right from the warm and bloody entrails of our own fighting men and women in the armed services*.

But—here's the fun patriotic punch line—the debts we owe the Chinese and other sovereign wealth funds are now worth approximately what the dollar is worth: crap! Less than puka shells!

So our debt payback is more like, "Um, kiss it, China."

We pulled a global economic Trump & Dump.

Want to do a hostile corporate takeover of America, China?

Well, we're going to fuck it up so bad *you don't even want it anymore*. Howdya like *that?*

But wait, it gets even better.

The privatization of services traditionally provided by the government pretty much exclusively benefits ambitious and well-connected corporations and their wealthy representatives. But the goal, of course (even though nobody explicitly talks about it because it's impolite), is the direct wealth-jacking of the middle class, and the siphoning off of all its benefits, pensions, pay raises, assets and equity (and free time spent not working), and giving all these to the extremely rich.

Because, after all, if the middle class got too rich, it wouldn't be the middle class anymore, now would it? No.

Boom. There, I said it.

But before you get on your high horse and condemn me as an elitist despot, know this: Your Divinely Elected Commander in Chief represents you. We are all accomplices.

For example: Due to the dictates of your capitalist economy and the corrupt mechanisms now set in the stone tablets of your national laws, you are already helping me kill small children on a daily basis. (See Diagram.)

We are *all* complicit in killing innocent baby children, every day, in one way or another.

You may not be holding the pitchfork in back of

HOW CAPITALISM KILLS INNOCENT CHILDREN:

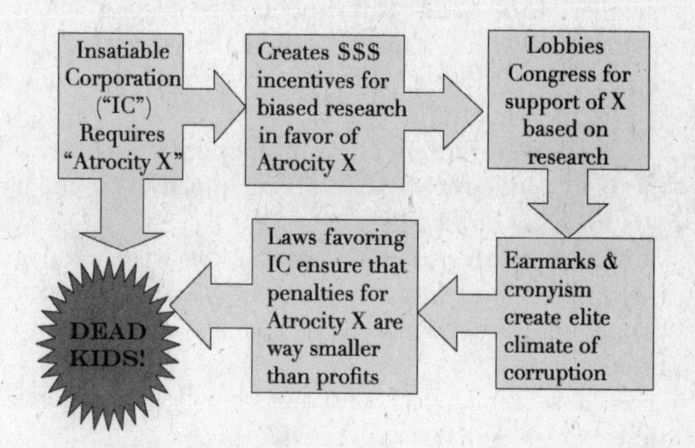

the dead-baby truck, but you have forfeited *your tacit consent* by not nonviolently hurling yourself in sacrifice in front of the pitchfork. As you see, we're all neck-deep in this warm slime together.

But, thankfully, the minute Britney (or her factual equivalent) shaves her tits on TV, none of that will seem very interesting, relevant or important.

We all break eggs. I've dealt with my baby killing in therapy, and I'm comfortable with it now.

As your divine Supreme Commander, I absolve you too.

Let's dispense with petty moralities, shall we? Let's slip out of our priestly drag into something a bit more comfortable, with feathers and a harness. A little outfit I like to call Econo-Fascisto-Oligo-Megolopolism.

At a certain point, the big dogs and I were all sitting around in our posh underground bunker, looking for a third world to rape, and one of us—I can't remember who—said, "I've got it! The biggest, most potentially rapable third world on the planet is right in our own backyard. In fact, it is our backyard."

Oh, the forehead slapping.

I sold off everything in my grandmother's palace to the Gauls—they were wild about imperial kitsch. It was the eBay of the SPQR.

A high tide raises all yachts, as it were. And a higher tide, like a tsunami, wipes out all the icky poor people on the coastline and enables developers to build resorts.

Because, remember: Who owns big global corporations?

Banks. Financial lending institutions.

Who owns banks? Small groups of rich people that actually run everything.

And actually, ME, within about twelve days of taking office.

We're going to revitalize the economy by electroshocking its vital signs back into beeping steadily, while, in reality, it will be as brain-dead as a bowl of coleslaw. We will keep it alive expensively on life support until all the harvestable organs are sold off.

Democracy is really terrible for aggressive free-market capitalism. Military dictatorships, on the other hand, are truly fab.

Let's think about Milton Friedman's Chicago School of Economics.

Friedman thought that the government shouldn't interfere with the economy.

Friedman proved that he was right, and Keynes was

wrong: There is no inverse relationship between the rate of inflation and the rate of unemployment. Remember the "stagflation" of the 1970s? America had high rates of both inflation *and* unemployment. This made Milton Friedman *very* happy. The Chicago School became very popular with Americans like Henry Kissinger.

Close adherence to the macroeconomic principles of the Chigago School was how we put the psycho-squeeze on Chile after the Pinochet coup in 1973. Since Chile was in danger of becoming (horrors!) *pinko-socialist*, Pinochet's appointees—actual members of the Chicago School, groomed by the United States—advised Pinochet to privatize banks, allow foreign imports and eliminate price controls. Inflation rose 375 percent in a year—hunger was rampant, unemployment was insane.

So what did Pinochet do?

He followed Friedman's advice *again*, and gutted government spending even *harder*. This is because Freidman said it would make Chile's wildly unstable new free market economy "equalize."

And so, after a few more years of global corporations cannibalizing Chile down to the hard, indigestible, horn-and-bone matter, Chile's economy completely collapsed.

Then everything had to be nationalized all over again.

Hey, that's sort of a victory for you commie-minded sorts, right?

As former Indiana basketball coach Bob Knight once said, "If rape is inevitable, relax and enjoy it."

Let the corporations have their way with you and your country for a while, and in the end, everything will "normalize" back to the way it was before they got there! Eventually, everything will be so trashed and pillaged it will need to be regulated by the government again!

Regulations naturally seep back in as "governors" on the unchecked corruption and unaccountable greed that flourishes when the free market is left to nakedly pursue its own appetites with no grown-ups or babysitters in the house. It's sort of like letting go of the steering wheel and flooring the gas pedal at the same time. It's really fun for a minute. Everybody wins.

Sort of.

Well, no, not really, but for my purposes, yes.

But wait, I want to rub your face in one last excellent way you've had your economic extremities cut off and fed to a select group of uncaring, invertebrate, ruling-class cucumbers with fangs and Spock ears.

Friedman pretty much trashed our adherence to the economic ideas of Keynes, who thought it was the federal government's responsibility to keep the economy alive during periods of recession and inflation.

We discarded all the hard, toothy parts we didn't like about Keynes, but kept one creamy nougat center bit that we did like: "Military Keynesianism."

This is where Enron-style, faith-based accounting really gets magically ridiculous. It's so good.

This is when your domestic economy *requires constant war* in order to justify bleeding dizzying trillions out of the future in unsustainable deficit spending.

I like to call Military Keynesianism "Nosferatu,

the Foreign Policy." It means we get to sneak around in the dark and wreak havoc all over dirty little countries, because we *have* to. *We need to drink their blood to survive.*

Military Keynesianism means the economy gets a sudden juice-boost of wildly unaccountable new defense spending. And here's the kicker: It requires that we keep up *sustained, prolonged and relentless military ambition* in order for the economy not to suck backward into itself and collapse like a Superdome-size water blister.

It's the economic plan endorsed by Germany in the 1930s and under former GE spokesman Ronald Reagan in the 1980s.

Once, during the New Deal, deficit spending was a means of transferring wealth to the jobless, old and desperately poor—like wretched old skanky welfare queens who wear midriff halter tops and mounds of cheap gold jewelry. But *now*—behold. Deficit spending, and the confiscation of wealth it represents, wealth that once was the social safety net for the less fortunate, is now transferred into the hands of the wildly super-duper aristocratic and otherwise obscenely fortunate!

You think you know what the Department of Defense is spending? The Department of Defense doesn't even know what the Department of Defense is spending. There's a hundred billion dollars stuffed into every janitors' closet, for projects nobody even remembers. There's stuff that *isn't even included in the Defense budget* that if you knew about, you'd feel like millions of tiny needles were erupting through your scalp. Hundreds of basquillions of your future taxpayer dollars are already spent on bizarre and inscrutable Homeland Security costs, new nuclear weapons and foreign arms sales so extensive that soon everyone over the age of seven will be able to invade Pakistan.

There isn't even a reliable *method* for the military to track its own costs—everyone just gave up at a certain point and watched the digits spin.

Capitalism, like feudalism and slavery before it, is the most enduring, insidious and compelling structure by which a parasitic minority of aristocratic families gets to monopolize life as you know it, and doom You People, the majority, to an insectoid life of debt slav-

THE IRON TRIANGLE | EXPLAINED

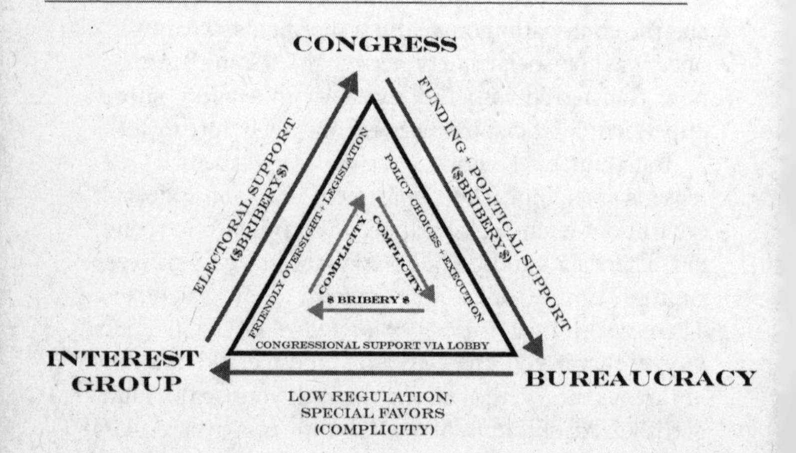

ery in office cubicles. In the last seven years you got drop-kicked out of the middle class and marginalized down to sharecropper status, where history dictates that you inevitably belong.

No need to wait and pray until the black smoke of negative amortizations starts creeping over the horizon toward your house. The hot winds bloweth toward thee, American citizen, for thou livest in an economic fire-corridor built on jittering fault lines, oil-soaked rags and 30 percent credit card interest rates—an outlandish vigorish, punishable by death in decent crime families.

Free trade is like whipped cream on tits if you're on the right side of the painted tape. And yes—it's incompatible with human decency.

Virtue is its own reward, they say. Actually, virtue is its only reward—you get to be really proud of yourself for being virtuous. Good for you. It's vanity, actually, and you're probably just a narcissistic loser who secretly thinks you're superior to everyone else on an invisible level that nobody else can see.

If you've achieved complete ass-out shamelessness, however, you can dispense with virtue quite easily. It's really very liberating, and crucial to great wealth in a free market.

It's not money that elevates some men over other men; it's moral agnosticism and the cleverness to use it to build small gangs of Thugocratic Pervo-Industrial Syndicalists, and commence with no-holds-barred international beat-downs. It's Thug Life Rex Lexus Dominus, baby. The sun never sets, the blood never dries, the party never stops . . . and I'm sorry, but please step away from the velvet rope if your name is not on the list . . . and I'm sorry, but you don't seem to be on the list, *China*.

Here's my bold economic plan:

We're just going to keep going with all the same tendencies here, only push them a little further, because the economy is an organism that is way bigger than the silly oversights and maths of man and beast.

I have my own macroeconomic theory.

I call it the Detroit Skool of Economixxx.

After a prolonged period of savage and total economic decline, triple-digit unemployment, massive debt defaulting and quadruple-digit inflation—a multipronged whammy of hits I call "stagflatioruptcy"—more ordinary young people will turn to our new social safety nets: prison and the military!

It's "Military Philippinesianism," and it's already happening.

Unless somebody figures out how to round up the entire federal government, the whole executive branch, the Department of Justice, the Department of the Treasury, select cliques in Congress, all the agencies in charge of regulation and oversight, all banks, Wall Street, most corporations, etc., etc., ad nauseum, and prosecute them under the Racketeer Influenced and Corrupt Organizations Act (RICO) statutes for conspiracy and racketeering, well . . . changing anything would basically require burning the entire country down and starting all over again.

But it's not all bleak!

Think of it this way: America is now the equivalent of a junk bond the size of the *Titanic*, hitting an iceberg the size of America.

Was there a bilge pump that might have saved the *Titanic*?

No.

But here's the good news: If America goes completely down, the sucking vortex will take almost all the other ships in the ocean down with it as well.

Plus! Here's my bonus New Deal plan for economic revival: In order to sidestep spiraling inflation, America requires a durable new commodity to serve as a medium of exchange—a new gold standard to restore the credibility of government-created bank credit.

Unfortunately, the Chinese have completely outclassed us in terms of gold ownership. So, we'll have to start getting creative with what we put in the United States Bullion Depository at Fort Knox. Along with the 4,570 metric tons of gold bullion, we should consider adding goods that Americans themselves consider to be our most valuable assets: Leroy Neiman prints, the Batmobile, sports memorabilia, and the virginity of Miley Cyrus.

That would put some meat back on the dollar and really make the nuns lose their lunch.

Fear will keep us safe. Remember, we're flying, not plummeting.

As Gerald Ford once said, "Our long national nightmare is over!"

A VALUABLE OFFER FROM CALIGUBANK

CALIGUBANK will send you checks from your available line of credit—with your own name printed on them. They're exactly like checks! Your very own checks, to spend however you want! They're extra cash for YOU, because YOU deserve it! For example, you can spend some valuable Me Time unwinding at a spa, buy a convertible and drive around wearing cool sunglasses . . . or, best of all, you can buy a Bose Wave CD player. Every time you open your CALIGUBANK credit card bill, there will be a little ad-reminder for the Bose Wave CD player, on its own special flap. CALIGUBANK couldn't possibly recommend it more highly, or often enough.

Have you ever experienced the thrill of seeing your own name in *raised letters* on a stylish CALIGUBANK card? We'll send you one. You can take it right out of your mailbox and brandish it around your home, fantasizing about the subtle one-upsmanship and prestige such a card will bring you.

If you call our toll-free number, you might take advantage of some of the other great CALIGUBANK offers, like mortgage, refinancing and home equity loan opportunities.

Rush me that genuine sterling and sapphire tennis bracelet, and make it snappy, Bangalore phone-jockey! I am holding in my hand a piece of rectangular plastic from CALIGUBANK with holograms on it, and I don't think I need to tell you what kind of awesome buying power it gives me.

Cash out your ROTH IRA! Fuck the penalties!

You're a sultan! You have a credit card, and an invitation from your friend CALIGUBANK to explore all your WILDEST DREAMS! Your ship has come in. The future is now. Don't think about Treasury bills, you pathetic little man. You could be snorting heroin in a Bentley upholstered in lynx fur.*

---

*CALIGUBANK investments are not insured by the FDIC.

8

BUILDING AMERICA'S DREAM-GULAG: HOMELAND SECURITY AND THE ART OF SUPPRESSING SLAVE REVOLTS

Fiat iustitia, et pereat mundus.
(Let there be justice, though the world perish.)
—Motto of Holy Roman Emperor Ferdinand I

We live in a society in which slavery isn't recognized. It's nevertheless clear to any sociologist or philosopher that it has in no way been abolished . . . Bondage hasn't been abolished, one might say it has been generalized.
—Jacques-Marie-Émile Lacan

Imperial Rome is the center of the Empire. An undisputed master of the world. But with this power inevitably comes corruption. No man is sure of his life, the individual is at the mercy of the state, murder replaces justice. Rulers of conquered nations surrender their helpless subjects to

bondage. High and low alike become Roman slaves,
Roman hostages. There is no escape from
the whip and the sword.
—Opening narration, *Quo Vadis*

These laws, having multiplied and atrophied over
time, are now so alien and inscrutable that a priest
class of lawyers makes a living off the rest of us.
—The anarchists

While we're making amendments to the Constitution, let's rephrase "Life, Liberty, and the pursuit of Happiness" and make it "life, liberty, and the pursuit of happiness (based on a conditional definition of happiness based on 'happiness' within the legally defined limits based on the subjective personal preferences and values of the ruling authority, who may not want to allow you to use recreational drugs or be openly homosexual or drive over 45 mph for whatever personal reasons they see fit)."

Leaders like me have learned a lot from the Catholic Church over the years. Laws are necessary to make you guilty. Punishments are extremely important to ensuring an absolute executive grip on your divine military authority.

In order to sufficiently frighten your public, you need sufficient threats and the divine will to carry them out. Historically, powers in charge have tailored these punishments to best terrify the populace according to the cultural beliefs of the time. When the Vatican had the entire world by its metaphysical jock and was keeping the bank trade alive by shaking people upside down by their own guilt-straps, heresy and excommunication were the weapons of choice to level at those who stepped out of line—especially since they were usually enforced by being tortured to death.

"God hates you now" is still a fantastic thing to make people believe if you really want to upset them.

When leaders make rules that are antithetical to human nature, the citizenry is forced into a state of unavoidable transgression. This makes You People easier to herd: big, clear ideological guidelines that you can't really help but run afoul of. They make you *feel* dirty, and then you act in skulking, hangdog ways, which make you easier to prosecute, since you're doing half the job yourself.

The Catholics are absolute geniuses at this racket and have seen amazingly little resistance over the years, especially when you consider how many centuries they've been openly working the same sadomasochistic slap-and-tickle act:

I've been a ba-a-a-ad boy, Hail Mary. (Whap!)

Thank you Lord, may I have another?

Tiberius had gotten fairly deranged toward the end of his reign, as I have said before. He liked a good witch hunt and gleefully brought anyone who rubbed his scales the wrong way up on charges of *laesa majestas*—a wildly open-ended and ambiguous charge generally interpreted to mean an offense of impiety against Tiberius. This charge, of course, was purposefully vague, and in place just for the purpose of vent-ing imperial spleen on anyone the emperor was keen to abuse, for reasons as irrational as general stupidity.

It short, *majestas* was a thrillingly useful legal cure-all and terrific threat to the populace; it eventually evolved into the crime of lèse-majesté—injury to the majesty.

Lèse-majesté is really fantastic. I am bringing it back immediately. This law dictates that I embody the incarnate MAJESTY of the United States of America—therefore, any insult to me will be legally interpretable as high treason. It's not even an antique law! In October 2007, a forty-seven-year-old man was fined four hundred euros in the Netherlands for calling Queen Beatrix a "whore" in front of a police officer and describing profane sex acts he wanted to do to her.

Why do I want such harsh and restrictive laws?

There are more than a few instances of unpopular leaders finding themselves torn limb from limb by angry mobs throughout history. There's only one thing worse than filthy ignorant poor people, and that's when great stinking hairy chinless mobs of them suddenly start doing things as a group.

Do not say, "Personally, I am as worthless as a bolt, but if I stop being an isolated bolt and start gathering with my equally undistinguished and boltlike neighbors, we are, collectively, a big sack of bolts that can hit things harder."

You are not a bolt. You are wonderful special individual with talents and hopes and dreams of great fortune, fame and luxury. You are going to sing on television and become rich beyond your wildest dreams just by writing upbeat affirmations on Post-its and sticking them on your bathroom mirror.

Are you getting a tingly feeling in your shorts, fantasizing about civil unrest, O college student?

Let me disabuse you of any notion of success: History has not been kind to this type of disaster. Nice things don't happen to people who get too friendly with the poor.

One hundred and thirty-four years before we hung an antislavery activist named Jesus out to dry, Rome was dealing with a joker by the name of Tiberius Gracchus (no relation to my uncle Tiberius). The Gracchi were not exactly trash—they were a rich and well-connected ruling family of bleeding-heart, aristocratic sops. Gracchus was the grandson of Scipio Africanus, who defeated Hannibal.

Gracchus, a veteran of the Third Punic War, got his pinafore in a tangle over the fact that legionnaires coming back from long war campaigns often returned to Rome only to find themselves homeless. Their farms, which were generally left in the hands of their wives and children, usually went bankrupt; these properties were then essentially "foreclosed on" and scooped up by wealthy landowners.

"The truth is that our soldiers fight and die to protect the wealth and luxury of others. They are called the masters of the world, but they don't possess a single clot of earth which is truly their own," bleated Tiberius Gracchus.

This kind of populist mob-speak got him elected tribune of the people—an office charged with protecting plebeians and their property. In 133 B.C. he began to champion the plight of homeless soldiers, appealing to the *mobile vulgus*—"the easily moveable crowd."

Needless to say, this really pissed off the senate, the dominant number of whom were rich landowners. Gracchus finally completely alienated them when he was able to push through a bunch of agrarian reform legislation benefiting the poor.

In response to this act of class disloyalty, the senate ganged up on Gracchus and stabbed him to death.

Because what the fuck was Gracchus thinking anyway? What did he want Rome to be—an ochlocracy? Rule by illiterate, grease-exuding mobs of angry turnip-people?

Idiot.

Let me discourage you openly from binding together in your misery and poverty and putting on Gothic mime makeup like the rock band KISS and wearing baseball uniforms and picking up bats and steak knives and trying to pull any gangland shenanigans on your Big Uncle Sam.

Instead, let us encourage you in the profitable exercise of xenophobia. Xenophobia—the ultimate economic panacea, the yellow brick road back to recovering the Great Emerald in the crown of empire: slavery!

Let's face it: Everyone needs a scapegoat.

Peons, do me a favor: Please keep abusing each other over differences of skin tone and absurdly tiny religious discrepancies. It's good for the country. Racism *needs to rise* in periods where slavery makes a comeback, because if all you simian-browed, atavistic gutter-plebes started cooperating, all of a sudden, you'd barbecue our prissy fannies in a hot ghetto second.

Vent your feelings of rage, powerlessness and futility . . . Just make sure you keep hitting people economically worse off than you are, and everything will be peachy.

What makes America truly great?

You are already enjoying slavery, you just don't know it yet!

Here's the thing—you don't really need to have *slavery* qua "slavery" to have slavery.

I mean, let's just not *call* it that.

No man wants to think of himself as a slave! Eew!

That's why how you say these things is so important.

The way you perceive yourself makes all the difference in the world. There is absolutely no need to be demoralizing when You People will feverishly support enslaving yourselves if it's just packaged cleverly and attractively.

An aggressive use of lubricating semantics is as persuasive as truckloads of pig iron leg cuffs. You can pretty much get the same great slavery results, more or less, with debt bondage, indentured servitude, serfdom, peonage . . . or really, just an extremely low minimum wage.

If your minimum wage, in our great global race to the bottom, is ridiculously small enough to be, technically, slavery . . . *but* it provides just enough that you might sleep in a van instead of on a sidewalk, you will probably see your poverty as temporary (and surely it is!). You will see your disgraceful poverty as being *your own fault*—and therefore within your power to change (and surely it is!).

This enables you to have greater self-esteem and delusions of caste. You will decide you are racially superior to, say, the Dominicans, or the autistics, who are seemingly helpless and incapable of improving their own plights.

Then you will vote a straight Republican Party ticket, in the hopes that someday you will be able to oppress Dominicans, autistics and people just like yourself.

Not for nothing do the great religious books of Judiasm, Christianity and Islam all have passages that condone slavery.

Deliverance from slavery is a running leitmotif, sure, but really—read a little deeper into the books and you'll find a common theme that real deliverance only happens after you're *dead*.

And that's only if you're *really good*.

The Catholics, despite ostensibly existing to brutally enforce Christ's message of peace, couldn't actually manage to strangle out a papal bull against slavery until 1435.

The Qur'an says it's just dandy to enslave non-Muslims, as long as they're prisoners of war. The prophet Muhammad owned a few slaves and even had a baby with one of them. Slave trafficking wasn't really even openly repudiated in Saudi Arabia until 1962, and in Oman and Yemen until as late as 1970.

You can *still* be a hereditary slave in Mauritania, even though they started bad-mouthing it in 1981, probably just to get other countries to shut up about it.

Now, before you get all "politically correct" and start beeping and booping and sending pink-haired university lesbians out into the street to protest my bold new domestic policy, think of it this way: Slavery is the natural, homeopathic antidote to *Communism*.

And if that logic doesn't do it for you, let me discourage you about the efficacy of slave rebellions, which are totally unsuccessful 99 percent of the time.

They have literally only worked once: in Haiti. That was it. The Haitians managed, finally, to boot the French off the island, but that was largely because Napoléon III's brother, Charles Leclerc, managed to catch yellow fever while leading the expeditionary force to retake Haiti for the French, and cacked.

Go ahead—escape to Haiti! You'll be free! You'll be rioting for food and eating dirt cookies, but you'll be free!

Mechanisms are already in place to suppress all future slave rebellions, because slave rebellions are an *abject* pain in the nuts. They really louse up the cogs of imperial progress.

Let me share some statistics from a handful of history's famous slave uprisings, just so you know what you're up against.

Let's take the First Servile War against the Romans in Sicily from 134 to 132 B.C., led by the charismatic Syrian rebel Eunus, a former slave who was credited with having magical powers. Two hundred thousand slaves joined in the uprising. Oopsie! No go: The leaders were captured and wiped out. Gong.

Oh, wait . . . how about the Second Servile War

from 104 to 103 B.C., also in Sicily? A group of deadbeats, who had been enslaved because of their debts to Roman tax collectors, volunteered to fight a German tribe to escape slavery. Then other slaves caught wind of this and joined up as well. They eventually were able to assemble an entire trained and equipped *slave army* with two thousand cavalry units and twenty thousand infantrymen.

No dice: Our man, consul Manius Aquilius, thromped them into wet meat.

But gosh, Caligula, what about the THIRD Servile War from 73 to 71 B.C.? How did that one turn out? Gee, wasn't that one led by the great gladiator-general Spartacus himself?

Well, kids, Spartacus was able to assemble a band of escaped slaves that eventually swelled into a marauding band of over 120,000 mouth-breathing dung stackers who thought it was fun to aimlessly wander around raiding Italy. So, Rome sent out eight legions under the direction of a really type-A tycoon bastard named Marcus Licinius Crassus (literally ranked eighth by *Forbes* in its 2008 Top Ten Wealthiest Figures in History list, right between Henry Ford and Cornelius Vanderbilt). Crassus, with the help of another tight-ass general by the name of Pompey, finally trapped Spartacus and his dirty little armies and heel-kicked the throbbing giblets out of them.

Spartacus went down; Crassus then went about merrily crucifying the six thousand or so survivors, just to completely salt that field of hope.

Pompey and Crassus then used the threat of their legions to tilt elections, became consuls in 70 B.C. and went on to have very nice and powerful political careers because everyone loved them for restoring slaves to the cowering, dehumanized and servile state that masters prefer.

In the United States of America, of course, you have your own colorful history in this regard.

America's best slave uprisings were really tragic because they were, more often then not, unplugged by *other slaves*. Probably under torture, but still.

Let's see—there was Gabriel's Rebellion in 1800, which was rained out the night they had planned it, so they postponed it . . . during which time, two slaves snitched Gabriel out to their master, who told the governor, who called out the state militia. Gabriel tried to escape, but two other slaves ratted him out for the reward money (which they didn't even end up getting the full amount of). Gabriel, his two brothers and twenty-four of his coconspirators were hanged by the neck until dead.

Oh, let's see . . . 1811. The largest slave revolt in American history. Charles Deslondes led the revolt in Louisiana. Five hundred slaves went down the Mississippi River road on their way to New Orleans, burning a few plantations along the way and stealing weapons. But a planter militia, supported by United States troops, managed to kill a big chunk of them in an armed confrontation. Deslondes and the twenty slaves captured with him were sentenced to death and their heads were put on poles, just in case other slaves got the same hot idea.

Beginning to see a pattern here? Armies never quite seem to represent the underdog, now do they?

Then there was good old Denmark Vesey and his coconspirators in 1822, who thought they could seize Charleston, South Carolina. Nope. Snitched out before anything could even start. Tried, convicted, iced by your ever-loving government for your protection.

Suppressing rebellions is easy, for the simple reason that most slaves just don't *want* to stop what they're doing, kill the boss and become fugitives. Freedom is too abstract a concept: You can't eat it, fuck it, sit under it when it rains or even do very much with it besides get in trouble and have it taken away from you again.

Most sensible people like restrictions. Frankly, if Mother Jones wanted to pull a repeat of her 1903 performance today and march to demand a fifty-five-hour work week for child laborers, she'd probably be bitten to death by the very children she was trying to save.

Oh, peasant uprisings? Forget it. Those are even *lamer*.

Remember the slaughter of Frankenhausen? I don't, but apparently five thousand farmers, inspired by Martin Luther's plucky spirit of anti-Caesaropapism, decided to revolt against the Thuringian aristocracy in 1525. Even Luther didn't support these potato-drilling maroons. Tra-a-a-agic.

But for any of you commie pinko anarcho-socialist runts who still think a nice revolution will let you redistribute wealth according to your grubby little whims, I've got two words for you: PARIS COMMUNE.

France in 1870 was not unlike America today in that the gap between rich and poor was pretty much a bottomless abyss with flames coming up from it. In

France, however, there also wasn't enough food, and the military had just gotten their kidneys spooned out by the Prussians. Finally a bunch of proto-social democrats in Paris—a citizens' militia of hundreds of thousands calling themselves the National Guard—decided to rebel against the German Empire's provisional government, led by Adolphe Thiers.

After a brutal little scuffle with the National Guard over some cannons lying around Montmartre, Thiers and his forces scrambled to collect their wits in Versailles, and Paris became a Commune for a hot moment.

They really didn't do a bad job. They went about rather quickly doing highly idealistic stuff like granting equal rights to women and declaring an "international brotherhood"; schoolchildren were clothed and fed for free, church was separated from state; debts were postponed, the interests on them were abolished, and workers were allowed to take over businesses abandoned by their owners—who, the workers virtuously decided, would receive compensation.

The Commune was a veritable idyll until the Man, in the form of Thiers and the National Assembly's army, stomped the idealistic lugnuts out of them and executed twenty thousand people in one week. Some say thirty thousand. Some say fifty thousand.

Paris was under martial law for five years, after that.

To paraphrase Lenin: The Communards failed because they were pussies who weren't ruthless enough. Lenin, too, thought they really should have gone all the way and exterminated the ruling class.

But see, that's the beautiful part—they *couldn't*,

because that would have rubbed their ethically superior *ideals* the wrong way. (Snicker. Love your invisible handcuffs, brother! They're the sweet kiss of Jesus!)

Don't worry, though, beloved citizens. You will never have to make such a dreadful moral decision. I am going to protect you from anything like that ever happening in America.

I am going to declare martial law *immediately*, the very *second* I seize office. I realize that's kind of redundant, in that you already *are* under a de facto martial law.

All I really have to do, when I take power, is *not* make you *not* under martial law.

The Senate is seriously canoodling with, and looks like it is about to pass, the Violent Radicalization and Homegrown Terrorism Prevention Act of 2007 (S. 1959), a companion piece of legislature that attaches to the House bill, the Violent Radicalization and Homegrown Terrorism Prevention Act of 2007 (H.R. 1955), which sailed through the House of Representatives in October 2007.

I like to call S. 1959 what the lefty bloggers call it: the "Thought Crimes Bill."

Penned by Congresswoman Jane Harman (D-California), the chair of the House Homeland Security Subcommittee on Intelligence, the bill says some very disparaging things about your great Dumpster of information in the sky:

> The Internet has aided in facilitating violent radicalization, ideologically based violence, and the homegrown

> terrorism process in the United States by providing access to broad and constant streams of terrorist-related propaganda to United States citizens.

(Even though you mostly use it to look at porn.)

This bill is worded ambiguously enough to drive a lot of Joe McCarthy–style buses through—buses that civil liberties activists fear will be filled with civil liberties activists and driven to dark, underground domestic Gitmos.

> The term "homegrown terrorism" means the use, planned use, or threatened use of force or violence by a group or individual born, raised, or based and operating primarily within the United States or any possession of the United States to intimidate or coerce the United States government, the civilian population of the United States, or any segment thereof, in furtherance of political or social objectives.

This definition of "force" has some stoned hippies worried, since it is intended to mean something other than "violence" . . . like intellectual persuasion, writings and peaceable assemblies deemed "radical" by a ten-member National Commission on the Prevention of Violent Radicalization and Homegrown Terrorism.

These bills broaden the wide-wide-open definition of "terrorism" to pretty much criminalize just about everything you can think of that passes for dissent: political activity, protest by dissident groups, civil disobedience and nonviolent direct action; they would also support putting superspooky "Centers of Excellence" on college campuses, so that the excellent members of these centers might study the formation of burgeoning radical movements and rat out their fellow students like excellent Hitler Jugend.

Remember, paid informants are part of nature and the infinite variety of the animal kingdom.

Anyway, swizzle all those mandates together into a cocktail with a few other highly classified signing statements, presidential directives and military commissions, and basically, you pretty much have an ironclad guarantee that all you have to do to get housed into a four-by-four-foot cement box with a single drill hole in it is *piss me off*.

Unless you are an immediate member of my entourage, or one of their close friends or an equally wealthy member of their family, sorry, but I must presume you are pretty much an "enemy combatant," and you can and will go down for whatever lame reason I feel like trumping up that day.

And the lamer the better.

The dumber and more obviously lame, the *more powerful you will know I am.*

I hear you with my superbionic divine ear. You're saying, "Great Father Caligula, we don't think we're under martial law. Things aren't that dark. We're still free American citizens and taxpayers."

Bless you. You are absolutely right, for several reasons.

1. Under martial law, the writ of habeas corpus would be suspended, thus depriving you of the Bill of Rights.

Of course, the Military Commissions Act of 2006

suspends habeas corpus, but the law is kind of squishy and vague as to whether or not it can be applied to You American People, and *you are perfectly right in assuming that it doesn't.*

After all, we American presidents have a deep and abiding belief in submitting to checks and balances of our authority by our friends in Congress.

2. The Posse Comitatus Act of 1878 forbids military involvement in domestic law enforcement without the approval of Congress.

Public Law 109–364, or the John Warner Defense Authorization Act of 2007 (H.R. 5122), signed by President Bush in October 2006, allowed the president of the United States to declare a "public emergency" and station troops anywhere in America—regardless of what the state governor or local authorities had to say about it. This was repealed in 2008, but Posse Comitatus was totally suspended for an exhilarating little chunk of the last presidency. You were flying that trapeze without a net for over a year, and *I bet you didn't even know it.*

How slippery the slope, eh? Even if you "trust" your president now, the die is cast—now *everyone knows* how the black magic works, and all it will take is one crazy bastard to roll America back to a pre-information age. Lights out!

3. Under martial law, the president is empowered to convene "military commissions" to try anyone he designates an "unlawful enemy combatant" and to hold them in secret detention indefinitely.

Not that this is anything like an abnormal thing for an American president to do. The Alien and Sedition Acts of 1798 sent people to jail just for criticizing the Adams administration.

During World War I, close to a thousand people were sent to jail for speaking out against the war, in violation of the Espionage Act and Sedition Act.

Right before World War II, the Smith Act was passed that we might better imprison radicals—i.e., Trotskyists and Commies—for organizing literature that conspired to overthrow the government.

But that doesn't make it martial law, as such. It just makes you much safer from the threat of becoming a mushroom cloud—*a mushroom cloud that would flash-fry your world into a radioactive crater full of quivering, phosphorescent cancer-Jell-O.*

By the way, U.S. Northern Command (USNORTHCOM) is a whole lot more directly involved these days with civilian administration stuff. Do you know what that means? Me neither. But it doesn't apply to you, probably, because you're not under martial law.

4. If you were already under martial law, you wouldn't be able to avail yourself of the justice guaranteed to you by the American legal system. Instead, you'd be subjected to a trial without representation by a military tribunal.

Again, you are perfectly right in your assumption that this doesn't apply to you American citizens. This only applies to "enemy combatants."

And maybe American citizens declared to be "domestic terrorists."

Bad people like the Unabomber sitting in his isolated toolshed, or Nazi skinheads, or kitten torturers like Timothy McVeigh or overweight Peace Moms in pink foam-rubber Statue of Liberty headbands. Or PETA.

Not *you*.

Yes, you *are* under surveillance, and your e-mails are being data-mined, and your phone calls are being tapped . . . But this is wartime, and it makes you feel safer from the terrible cancerous mushroom cloud.

5. This will make you feel even safer-safer: In 2005, the president discussed the use of the military as a means of quarantining areas of the United States in the event that they were infected with bird flu.

Bird flu is the new black plague!

"Buy plastic tarps and duct tape" is the new "buy lots of canned food and have a bomb shelter." Protect yourself against the horror of bird flu and soil yourselves in fear every time a swan dies in Portugal! The Centers for Disease Control ran some large pandemic control scenarios with professional war game experts, just to make sure we could keep you perfectly safe. And guess what?

We determined that we couldn't keep you perfectly safe yet.

So we are making secret classified plans to make you really especially perfectly squeaky-safe from the terrifying and evil bird flu.

Righteously indignant author Mike Davis rhetorically asked, "Is America going to become one single huge squalid Superdome under martial law if there were an avian flu epidemic?"

The answer is no, Mike, of course not. Chuckle.

Gosh Manhattan, you don't look so good. I think your tongue is coated. I think you might have the bird flu. Or maybe turkey pox. Or maybe galloping AIDS from meth-crazed homosexuals—perhaps the greatest single threat to the American way of life, aside from promiscuity-based rabies. And antibiotic-resistant cooties. And an epidemic of penis-shrinking by evil Wiccan sorcerers.

Just kidding.

You know what unequivocally proves you're not under martial law? You don't have a curfew. Of course, night-vision surveillance is so fantastically advanced now that curfews aren't actually necessary anymore.

I like to think of these "not quite martial law but actually sort of essentially the same thing as martial law" laws as the Quintus Fabius Maximus Strategy of Constant Harassment that keeps you mildly depressed, exhausted and incapable of any sustainable, organized, effective resistance.

Quintus Fabius Maximus, of course, was the general who chiseled away at Hannibal's attacks on the Italian peninsula for fifteen years, in a way that didn't actually defeat that elephant-schtupping Carthaginian meatus, but undermined his efforts just enough to keep him from *making any meaningful progress toward sacking Rome*.

Let's take the Transportation Security Administration as an example of my point. It's so diabolically fucked as to be a constant source of entertainment.

Here's what you don't understand about Homeland

Security. It isn't in place so that men with long black beards, unironed shirts and glassy shark-eyes can't blow up your public buildings or hijack commercial jets.

It's to keep You People as far away from me as humanly possible—and to make sure that if you do get anywhere near me, you're declawed, defanged, sniveling, frightened, ball-gagged, zip-cuffed and preferably shoeless.

Air travel used to be stylish and comfortable; now it resembles being processed and detained in a Soviet drunk tank—and *not for nothing*.

The 9/11 hijacking was done with knives. It was an act so atrocious that it was beyond the realm of the American imagination at the time. Nobody could believe anyone would do such a thing; it was so unexpected, so apparently random.

However, good things came out of it.

Now, every time you get on a plane, *you innocent American citizens who happen not to be flying private jets* are all reduced to being processed like rape suspects entering an internment camp, and forced to show unschooled rent-a-thugs your appendix and your sexual devices and whatever else they feel like looking at.

Often, armed military personnel are brought in to "confiscate" certain items of your property that are *obviously benign*—little personal luxuries like cigarette lighters, sealed bottles of wine and tiny, thirty-two-dollar pots of lip gloss.

The point isn't that these lip gloss containers might be cram-packed with napalm—they would still be completely harmless, even if you beat them against the fuel tank with a blowtorch. The point is to *ruin your day*, and gradually acclimate you to passively accept little invasions and seizures of your personal property, for your own protection (*snort*).

It's this steady drip-drip-drip erosion of your expectations that makes your life suck just a little harder every year in ways that annoy and depress you but seem reasonable enough not to provoke an actual rebellion.

It's just like boiling frogs.

When you are processed into labor and internment camps, where do you think we will be processing you?

The international airports, naturally! The security mechanisms, electric fences and guard towers are already in place!

Why else do you think all the airlines are failing?

Where do you think you're going?

We're actually doing this for ecological reasons.

Extraordinary renditions leave too much of a carbon footprint. In the interest of reduced emissions and protecting the environment, the United States will become one big black interrogation site. At any moment, we might find a dangerous domestic terrorist among you and protect America by taking you for a nice ride to the airport.

Be sure to bring your passport!

Oh, that's right—*you don't have one*.

You want one more little piece of evidence that the Transportation Security Administration isn't actually as concerned with your safety as it is acting in the sole interest of keeping angry plebian hordes away from me?

We're not telling you that when someone gets up and hijacks the plane, *everyone else on the plane should immediately gang up on him*, throw laptops, throw coffee, throw anything. Everyone should attack at once—even if the guy has a hostage—because one guy really can't fight 114 people. United Flight 93 proved that an alert citizenry could thwart terrorist ambitions by thinking fast and working together quickly *as a group*.

But this was too empowering to discuss, really. We don't want to encourage You People to swarm together and attack when you think you see something thuggy happening. Strength in numbers is *not* something you want to fuck around with.

And the good news is, you won't need to form such groups for any reason, to protect yourself from oppression by terrorists or even your corporate godhead employers.

I, Caligula, am pleased to announce an alternative "social safety net," which not only provides the undercastes with shelter, medical care and food, but also gives them gainful employment that is useful to society.

With an ever-increasing number of Americans choosing a life behind bars, mass incarceration is now offering a unique alternative to life "outside."

America proudly boasts the largest prison population in the world. The United States, home to 5 percent of the world's people, currently hosts 25 percent of the world's prison population: a whopping 2.3

million to 2.5 million incarcerated—roughly the population of Latvia.

Currently, 751 out of every 100,000 Americans are going to prison—a stunning 400 percent increase in the last twenty years.

Sixty-eight percent of these prisoners are nonwhite.

One third of the black male population now calls prison their home.

And they just keep coming back. The population of approximately four million ex-prisoners can't, after all, get jobs or loans, apply for federal housing or walk freely around ATMs, convenience stores and white ladies' handbags without arousing intense fear and suspicion . . . so a revolving door of recidivism is just what the doctor ordered!

The U.S. prison population is now so mind-blowingly huge as to be chronically immune to policy reform, so just to shake the whole thing up a little and give it a fresh coat of paint, I intend to bring back the old USSR-model gulag . . . but with more reality TV cameras!

Soviet labor camps weren't just for political prisoners—you could be trotted off to Siberia simply for unexcused absences from work, creating works of political satire or even telling an antiestablishment joke at a dinner party!

It's going to be so much easier to make prison your opportunity for a secure and protected future.

And let me let you in on a little secret as to why the new American gulag is going to be so popular. MSNBC has already done the math on this one: Prison = Entertainment! Now and forever!

You incarcerated people are all going to be *stars*. On *TV*.

NBC has already begun to invent a fantastic fall lineup.

Dozens of analysis shows are going "inside the minds" of serial killers. More shows are devoted to inmates in maximum-security lockdown with swastikas tattooed on their cheeks. Entrapment shows expose awful, sniveling pedophiles trying to visit decoy children they met online. And of course, along with enormously popular, long-running, real-life shows like *Cops,* there's a little something in the criminal justice community to entertain everyone in the family!

As a child in Rome, there was nothing I loved more than seeing the prisoners of war marched through town, to be dressed in bloody animal skins and subsequently dismantled by wild dogs.

One of my big dreams is to bring back the good old public execution. If we are going to kill people, we should at least let all our citizens watch it on television, so they can be sexually aroused by it.

There is no greater aphrodisiac than capital punishment.

What do you think Henry Kissinger really had on his mind when he was talking about power?

Any asshole can have a black Lincoln town car. The ability to bed quality Hollywood trim like Jill St. John came from the fact that he could wave his fat little hand and *kill Cambodia*.

Major TV networks will compete to televise my creative new public executions the way they do for the Super Bowl.

Why should I stop there? North Korea's Kim Il Sung tests chemical weapons on his prisoners. What about this, exactly, wouldn't goose prime-time ratings?

You may be wondering why I insist that you want to be slaves, and/or in jail, and stars on TV.

I will level with you.

Although American democracy is based on principles of freedom . . . you actually *hate* freedom. You find it *intolerable.* You're *terrified* of it.

When moral freedom is given to you, you cage yourself with the dogma of religion. When sexual freedom is available to you, you wrap it in black latex, verbally abuse it, stick a ball-gag in its mouth and hit it with Ping-Pong paddles.

You don't like wild people any more than you like wild animals—they're too unpredictable!

But you love to see them contained in zoos, and buy cute, miniaturized, plush velour versions of them. You find freedom repellant, but you adore monuments honoring dead freedoms. Taxidermized panthers in attack pose. Laws that eliminate the very freedoms they are ostensibly written to protect. Dead Jesus on a stick.

I promise you'll be able to purchase plush velour versions of death row inmates to your heart's content.

Prison is truly the place for you.

I will make you feel *really punished* and you can wallow in a luxurious splendor of self-pity and pious repentance. I will gleefully deprive you of all food but "nutri-loaf." You will be forced to distill your own "pruno" to get a buzz on, and construct revolting, lotion-filled "fifi bags" to simulate intercourse.

Just think: You can utterly lose control when we lock you in "the box" and piteously reenact that scene from *Raging Bull* where De Niro fights himself, with cameras watching you and an entire audience being moved by your plight. Ready for your close-up?

Don't tell me that doesn't sound fun.

Absolute Leadership really comes down to nerve, and a willingness to wear the black gloves.

At some point, you would have to fire-hose a large batch of civic-minded college students for no good reason other than the base flexing of might.

At some point, you would have to confront a weeping crowd led by a brainlessly unrealistic but popular ideologue with legitimate gripes (like "Peace Mom" Cindy Sheehan, who lived in a ditch and sniveled into a bullhorn outside Bush's Crawford ranch for the better part of 2006, or the "Bonus Army" of seventeen thousand disgruntled veterans who marched against Herbert Hoover), and you would have to make the unpopular decision to trot out the National Guard and shoot them.

Instead of murdering your betters, think of your nation as the Austrian father who loved you so much he couldn't bear to share you with the rest of the world, planned your dungeon captivity for years in advance, then took you away from the influence of sunlight when you turned eighteen and kept you there until you were forty-two.

Stockholm syndrome is a much easier and nicer way to go, for everyone involved. Love is the answer!

Though I am your greatest natural enemy, I prance

carelessly through the valleys of deepest Nowheresville, USA, and I have no fear. Do you know why?

Do you know what the greatest threat to you is?

You.

Ever since phones became cameras, you have been policing yourselves like little state troopers. If by some miracle any of you are doing anything *remotely* interesting, you take great pains and expend your own time and meager personal resources to *post your doings on the Internet in the desperate hope that someone will pay attention to you.*

You put cameras in your own bedrooms. The outlaw-minded among you even *tattoo yourselves for easier identification and openly declare your radical, dissident beliefs on Facebook*. It's too good to be true.

You humiliate yourselves, and watch yourselves humiliating yourselves, and humiliate each other, and watch each other humiliating each other, as if you were all collectively re-creating the trauma of governance by an abusive authority. It's so cute.

Don't fight it—it's natural.

The problem really isn't that we, your Divine Ruling Authority, are trying to watch and police your every move; the problem is that *we're bored out of our minds because you all demand so much attention.*

I understand that many of you are concerned about the future of your privacy and the steady (and, may I add, largely *voluntary*) erosion of your civil liberties.

But seriously, check out YouTube. There's absolutely

nothing less interesting than your sex life, your e-mails and your phone conversations. I know. I've seen them.

Get a couple of national security heavyweights and telecom CFOs together over a tray of gelatinized Pucker shooters, and believe me, the evening *always* devolves into an invasion of your privacy, listening in on transmissions from those little orange box-rooms connected to AOL and Verizon.

Yawn.

Trust me, even at your most private, kinky or subversive moments, 99.9999 percent of you are duller than a fourteen-hour muscular dystrophy telethon.

I hate to break this to you, but these laws, which may seem draconian, aren't even really necessary, because—bottom line—you're already too well trained and mentally enslaved to have enough organizational power to mobilize anything truly subversive.

Oh, oh, look out: MySpace is going to put together a *march*. On the streets! With big banners! Saying, STOP, BAD GOVERNMENT! STOP DOING THAT BAD, BAD THING!

Hold me, Mother! We must, as a governing body, stop doing immoral things immediately, or bisexual college girls with nose rings might wave colorful signs at us!

Or worse yet!!

www.I_Hate_Caligula/blogspot.com has posted a scouring criticism of my governing methods!

Gahhh! My eyes . . . they burn! My laptop touch pad finger . . . is . . . turning . . . to salt!

No! *No-o-o-o-o!*

A popular sketch comedy group on a premium cable channel has satirized my foreign policy! I fall from darkness into darkness! All is lost!

I tremble in my open-toed wing tips (while Ito, my adorable Japanese houseboy, gives me a mani-pedi in the solarium).

Such efforts are visibly pointless, because if ubiquitous media conglomerates refuse to pay any attention to them, they really don't exist.

Do "demonstrations" exist if the people you're demonstrating your dissent to can't be buggered to notice?

It's theoretical: What if you threw an orgy and nobody came?

Short of monk-immolating or mass hunger strikes or armed rebellion . . . sorry, but *GONG*. Please evacuate the public arena so that something interesting can happen.

And please take your touchingly naïf, tempera-paint, cardboard, dry-macaroni-and-Elmer's-glue, second-grade art brut protest signs with you.

Thanks!

9

A HELLO TO ARMS; OR, ETERNAL WAR FOR ETERNAL WAR; OR, CATCHING YOUR DICK IN THE ZIPPER OF IMPERIAL OVERREACH

Bellum omnium contra omnes
(War of all against all)
—Thomas Hobbes

Oil is much too important a commodity
to be left in the hands of the Arabs.
—Henry Kissinger

Your empire is nothing but an old maidservant,
accustomed to being raped by everyone.
—Napoléon Bonaparte, to Austria

Fuck your parliament and your constitution.
America is an elephant. Cyprus is a flea. Greece is a
flea. If these two fleas continue itching the elephant,
they may just get whacked by the elephant's
trunk—whacked good . . . If your Prime Minister

gives me talk about democracy, parliament
and constitutions, he, his parliament and his
constitution may not last very long.

**—Lyndon Johnson to the Greek ambassador,
concerning Johnson's plan for settling
a dispute with Cyprus**

America is now the largest and most far-flung militarist dominate since the Holy Roman Empire, maintaining 737 military bases in 130 countries across the globe. And that's only counting the ones we openly gloat about, with flashy, showboating Roman-consul-style regional commanders keeping their hands firmly around the neck of the whole planet at NORTHCOM, SOUTHCOM, PACOM, CENTCOM, EUCOM and now AFRICOM.

It is generally agreed that man is a political animal. Hobbes thought that man's pre-political state of nature was a state of war. War, according to Carl von Clausewitz, is "a continuation of politics by other means."

I say war is the ecstatic fusion of manliness and beastliness, and politics is really just how we build the rationalizations and pretexts to declare it. Ultimately, all political energy serves a driving, primal need to reconnect with our original and most authentic selves through murder and looting.

You are born into a social contract: It is tacitly understood that you will obey the sovereign, i.e., ME, in exchange for me "protecting" you—i.e., not killing you.

This deal has been in place ever since the first caveman held a pointy rock to the temple of a smaller caveman, and has only been amplified since.

This is natural.

Whine all you like about how things have gotten worse over the last fifty years because of the insatiable greed and duplicity of the fundamentalist military-industrial complex churches of **WARIUS©**, but really? It's just pointless and dangerous to joust razor-sharp windmills. Any idiot knows that the first thing you do when seizing absolute power is *bribe the Praetorian Guard.* It's really the only tenured and tacitly understood method of making the cogs of accession mesh smoothly. First you hand out big fat bonuses to the military, then seize your power by force, then build your consensus via relentless intimidation and bondage attire.

Authoritarian military dictatorships have always been run on rude will, cold steel and leather pants.

Some of you may be saying to yourselves, "Caligula, this is a time when America should explore all diplomatic options. We can't get into more wars. We're dead broke, our armies are threadbare. We are already suffering from imperial overreach. We are insufficiently supporting the wars we already have going on."

Ding-dong, you're wrong! Wrong, wrong, wrong, wrong, dead wrong.

The bigger the empire, the more hardcore and aggressive its military dictatorship needs to be, in order to enforce its infernal bureaucracy all over the place.

America's empire isn't big enough yet, and neither am I.

In Virgil's *Aeneid*, Jupiter orders the founding of an *imperium sine fine*—"empire without end." Aeneas founded Rome, the "everlasting empire."

And it *was* sort of everlasting, until we fucked it up.

But now, together, we have a second chance.

America: This is SPARTA!

Well, no, not exactly. But let's call it *Manifest Destiny 2.0: The Wonder Years.*

Once upon a time, a long, long time ago, for a century preceding the Roman republic when the tyrannical Etruscan kings worried the wolf-tits off the Roman people, the Etruscan symbol of leadership was a fasces, a big staff of birch whipping-rods, all tied together with a double-bladed ax, which signified both the leader's ability and willingness to either lash Roman citizens into pulpy matter, or—better yet—simply whop their heads off. The fasces is the ultimate symbol of corporal punishment and/or potential head-removal, thereby symbolizing the ultimate exercise of executive power.

During times of peace, the ax was traditionally rearranged so the blade faced inward, or it was taken out. Then the ax would be put back in as the dictatorial powers of wartime were declared. It symbolized that the leader had become aggressive for a reason.

Anyway, Rome's obedience to the Etruscan fasces all came to a halt when Sextus, the son of Etruscan king Tarquinius Superbus, raped a chick named Lucretia who was a member of a distinguished and noble Roman family. This was the last straw: All the rich people in Rome financed a revolt, and the Etruscans haven't been heard from much since. Rome adopted the fasces as a symbol for its own centurions.

Rome hated tyrants after that, and remembered that it hated tyrants for four whole centuries, until it forgot and the clock went back to zero again.

Italian fascism got its name from the fasces, Benito Mussolini being a tastemaker who knew a good instrument of oppression when he saw one.

The fasces evolved from its original ancient symbolic meaning to now symbolize something akin to "United We Stand" (only with an ax in the middle).

Or so you *think*.

There is a fasces, hanging right now, in the Oval Office, above the door leading to the president's private office, a few of them scattered around the Lincoln Memorial and really a whole lot of them wherever you find a whole bunch of power densely concentrated in an exclusive roomful of white men, like the Senate and the House of Representatives, and on Nazi postage stamps.

As your Holy American President, I am proud to proclaim that your American Dominate is now fully ax-out, 24-7-365. The ax is back, and sharp enough to shave with. The fasces has been restored to its original meaning . . . tyranny! And the ax will never face inward, ever again.

There was a responsible leader named Cincinnatus, once. He was a landowner who, in a time of war and crisis against a dangerous tribe, was granted absolute

THE FASCES IN OUR WORLD

COLORADO FASCES

DIME FASCES

HOUSE OF REPRESENTATIVES FASCES

KNIGHTS OF COLUMBUS FASCES

HITLER FASCES

power of dictator to lead Rome. He accepted it, took up arms and smeared the offending Germans. Then he *resigned* after two weeks and returned to his farm. He gave the power *back*.

A statue of Cincinnatus, in Ohio, shows him giving back the fasces after his war was over.

Absolute power. He. Gave. It. Back.

Thanks, Rome! Don't need it anymore. Going back to my plow. Cheers.

What a *twat*.

After World War II was over, the American military was supposed to get smaller again. The Pentagon—no lie—was supposed to be turned into a large storage container. But instead of giving the fasces back, so to speak, the military just kind of moved in permanently and began overjustifying its existence.

Likewise, after the fall of the Soviet Union in 1989 when the cold war was over, the military—again, instead of getting smaller—took peace as its cue to get exponentially more enormous.

This could be because diplomacy is great, and very important when you're caught in bed naked with your proconsul's wife, but really—killing people is the most efficient solution for everything.

Economic issue? Kill. Political issue? Kill. Cultural issue? Kill.

Central to the idea of a democracy is the ruse that civilian control of the military prevents military dictatorships. But it's different when the civilians running the defense establishment are oil barons, arms manufacturers, spooks and spokesmen for General Electric. Former military leaders run the NSA and the CIA and sit on the boards of directors at virtually all private defense manufacturing corporations and intelligence services. Not that this affects their thinking in any way.

Not that *influence* is any kind of quantifiable or commodifiable payola. Or that vast sums of money in terms of year-end bonuses is any kind of *incentive*.

But I must say, it is truly *the tits* down here in the gilded bunkers of Shadow Government Land. We've got *everything*.

Whether our policies relate to domestic surveillance, coercive interrogation, invading sovereign nations, extraordinary rendition or just plain investing-fuckloads-of-cash-that-could-be-used-to-repair-roads-and-feed-schoolchildren-on-newfangled-electronic-death-gadgets-

and-invasions-of-your-privacy-and-cyber-chimps, you can bet your bottom dollar that we just spent your bottom dollar.

The beautiful thing is that we don't even have to admit to doing anything grimy anymore.

Now we are able to subcontract most of the nation's gamier atrocities to private mercenaries—who exist in a magical, nebulous corporate universe beyond laws or the reach of prosecution on any soil whatsoever, and therefore don't have any checks and balances either. Mercenaries don't worry so much about the things that get our volunteer army all confused and upset: honor, duty, valor, heroism, dignity, *blah blah blah*.

Mercenaries have missions that *don't exist*. Pouf!

Accountability?

Um, for what, Missus Hippy-pants?

Mercenaries know they're hired contract killers, and they don't *expect us* to care about them—or to have any moral imperative whatsoever. Believe me, this is so much more honest. It really is worth a few dollars more from the vantage point of the throne when you need a quick assassination or five not to have to deal with whether this is the "right thing to do" or not.

"Nervos belli, pecuniam infinitam," as we used to say. Endless money forms the sinews of war.

Imperial expansion can basically be viewed as a pure expression of the unbridled id of the leader—a total disregard for boundaries either personal or geopolitical, based on executive privilege. The nation's military serves at the pleasure of the pleasure-seeking executive, for pleasure.

L'Etat, c'est moi, baby. Do not look directly at me!

The state is me, the land and I are one. With executive power this hashish-concentrated, you bet your ass that any aspect of my character, defect or virtue, is going to be played out *very broadly* on the world stage—and I really don't care which.

You don't believe that the consequences of power concentrically emanate in the character of the character that wields it?

Well . . . has America been behaving like a recovering alcoholic much lately?

Hmm, let's see—the USA got obese and insufferable, lost all its friends, position, hope, cash, dignity and moral compass; shaved its head and drove drunk around the globe with no panties; called itself the Antichrist; abandoned its children, totaled its SUV and keeps getting slapped around in the great parking lot of the Persian Gulf, because it refuses to go home.

So *what*. You gummy little tweens think this type of thing is new?

Andrew Jackson used to beat people with a hickory cane until they couldn't move anymore. Andrew Jackson was a ruthless expansionist who actually *enjoyed* killing Indians.

His pal James Polk was an unregenerate slave owner, who beat Mexico like a piñata in order to steal California in 1846—allegedly because he wanted to expand slavery into the Southwest.

Lyndon Baines Johnson enjoyed urinating in sinks and exposing his private parts. Some recently declassified documents reveal that the Johnson administration faked the Gulf of Tonkin incident, which gave America her juicy pretext for bombing North Vietnam.

Jack Kennedy liked having sex with three girls a day. He would shamelessly walk over and "simply pull girls' dresses up," according to his friend Lem Billings.

I fuck my sisters. A *lot*. All the time. Because I *can*.

Unipolar! That is how the axis of power should be. Jealousy is what the concentration of powers is all about. Don't hate the playa, hate the game.

I realize you think that wars of choice and conquest are superfluous when you're all broke from various high-level bank scams and essentially fraudulent health insurance . . . not to mention incurably dumb from having your brain mashed down to a factory-class sludge at St. Crackerburg Junior College.

According to Dr. Chalmers Johnson: "The most serious problem under [Emperor] Octavian was that the army had grown too large and was close to unmanageable. It constituted a state within a state, not unlike the Pentagon in the United States today."

True enough, but it is terribly important to a militaristic society to have constant wars going on that are both unwinnable and completely futile, in order to justify a constant running fire-hose blast of deficit spending.

For example, I personally vow that the United States will be running full-scale wars against both Drugs and Terror until both Drugs and Terror are completely obliterated from the earth.

These are big problems, sure. But don't tell me about asymmetric warfare: I fought the fucking *ocean*.

Seriously.

OK, look—I am going to come clean. I am going to share something with you.

I got a little too high once and tried to annex Britain. It was more or less my Bay of Pigs.

I guess I had taken to wearing my Alexander the Great costume a little too often. God, it's still embarrassing, almost two thousand years later!

Anyway, campaigns were a great party—we were basically drunk the whole time. We had these hilarious oratorical competitions where the loser had to erase the thing he'd just read with his tongue, or else we would beat him up with sticks and hurl him into the Rhône.

So, Britain. Here's what happened: We got to the shores of the English Channel somewhere around Boulogne, and then we set out in a trireme toward Britain—and the Channel was just so fucking cold and choppy and hard to cross that we basically chickened out, turned the thing around and went back to France.

A total boner, but did I let on? *No!*

I had my soldiers do some aggressive beachcombing, claimed the whole mess as an enormous victory against King Neptune and brought great loads of seashells back to Rome to prove it to the citizenry!

America killed the ocean too—it just took a lot longer.

It doesn't really matter what you tell people, as long as the wheels keep turning the right way.

Until we claim victory against the evil nouns of *Drugs* and *Terror*, tens of thousands of Americans will die every decade. Full stop.

And just to make the domestic psy-war skullfuck against you even more gratuitously painful, I intend to pronounce a "Mission Accomplished" in the War on Drugs . . . and then never actually stop fighting the War on Drugs.

I will formally announce my triumph, cover myself with OxyContin tablets and ride down the Washington Mall in a chariot pulled by meth addicts, dispensing handfuls of generic Percocet to the citizenry. And then I will have you all arrested for unlawful possession of controlled substances.

The War on Terror celebration might be a little more complicated to pull off, but I'm sure it's nothing a decent Super Bowl halftime organizer couldn't pull together with a top-ranked gymnastic cheerleading team and a school bus full of ammonium nitrate.

It's called *winning*.

Yes, it's also called *cheating*.

But, like steroids in baseball, infidelity, drunk driving, petty theft and hitting your children just a little too hard, it's something that we all learn not to internalize for the sake of preserving the big picture.

If you want an empire, you need to turn your nation into an ear-biting cage-fight grappler. There's only one thing that keeps your colonies, vassal and nanny states in check, and that is constant brutality, wholesale massacres, wars of choice and wars of conquest.

This is basic Imperial Bastard Behavior 1A.

We *need* tributary states and/or protectorate nations. They are our little bitch zones: the equivalent of the pretty guys who braid our hair in prison.

These lands are indispensable for housing our

Pervo-Slumvakian sex workers, our hardest-working sweatshops, our biggest offshore accounts, our seizable corporate assets, tax shelters, drug cartels, weapons containers . . . You get it.

Yes, it's a corporate-military model of government, and has been for quite a while. Get over it.

You People should learn to appreciate the bitter grown-up taste of safety, because it's *really fancy and expensive.*

Just as other great American presidents have done, I will make it one of my first acts to bestow a massive fortune in tribute and alms on the altars of **WARIUS©**. May the War God's earthly representatives Raytheon, Boeing, Northrop Grumman, McDonnell Douglas, etc., be sated in their love for new robots and machinery laden with fascinating electronic gadgetry, and therefore require fewer human sacrifices!

Some of you have written in to ask, "Gee, Caligula, how come we've been at war in Iraq for five years and there are no F-22s there?"

Well, that's because F-22s are so expensive they're basically a Ferrari. You don't want to drive it on the road because you might get hit by somebody.

It doesn't matter—we need to build all kinds of things we're not actually going to use so we can sell them to smaller countries later. As Lex Luthor said in *Superman Returns*: "Whoever controls technology controls the world."

I'm allocating seventy million dollars in congressional earmarks and emergency war spending to have the Defense Advanced Research Projects Agency

(DARPA) develop bionic combat pandas as the ultimate weapon against China. Everyone knows the Chinese love pandas. Just think how great it will be when the adorable, revered pandas start invading elementary schools and blowing sarin bubbles out their ears, and the Chinese are forced to exterminate their most beloved endangered species.

That's *drama.*

It will be even more spectacular than when my two-ton, cylindrical, uranium-coated tungsten "Rods from God" are GPS-guided down from my Divine Retribution Satellite to Malibu and turn David Geffen's compound into a black silt the consistency of Cream of Wheat.

Polonium 210? It's not just for Russian journalists anymore.

Don't go to any family restaurants in New Hampshire. That's all I'm going to say.

The threat of an endless struggle against Global Islamo-Petroleo-Fascism is, for us boys with military-industrial interests, sort of like a being given an open bar and an all-you-can-eat bacon buffet at the Playboy Mansion.

Former president Jimmy Carter perhaps said it best, in 2006: "The reason that we went into Iraq was to establish a permanent military base in the Gulf region."

Yes, Jimmy.

Because oil is liquid strategic power. Because tanks and planes eat it.

This is news? This is some kind of *revelation*?

The Middle East contains two thirds of the world's oil reserves. *Of course* we want uninterrupted access to the wonderful reserves of light crude in Iraq. Of course we are spending zillions—not on the "reconstruction" of Iraq as a free "democratic" society for actual Iraqi "people," but on *permanent military bases* and a fantabulous spend-o-gasm of a showplace embassy-fortress that I like to call "Chateau Honky."

Because I like to pause before a fucking reflecting pond. For *reflection*.

My *own*.

We've got a Global War to Defend Civilization Against Atavistic Takfiro-Fascism to fight, now and forevermore.

We are on a crusade to prevent Islamo-fascisto-fundamentalism by replacing it with a good, old-fashioned, Western-style corruption that benefits ME. Installing a lousy son-of-a-bitch and keeping him on a choke-chain isn't a perfect system, but it beats the hell out of trusting anyone with free will.

The first thing Hitler did the minute he got the opportunity was burn down the Reichstag, blame it on the Communists and put Germany under martial law for its own safety.

Then, of course, there were those hijinks in Gdansk, or Danzig, as it was known at the time.

The Danzig post office was located in one of those *Twilight Zone*, extraterritorial areas granted to Poland under the Treaty of Versailles.

But the Treaty of Versailles was a real cock-block for Hitler, so he just ignored it—sort of the way we ignore the Geneva Conventions, or the Treaty of Westphalia or the writ of habeas corpus.

Germany required an "incident" on the border as a pretext for invading Poland, so it launched an attack on the Gdansk post office, which was armed to defend itself against what the Poles figured was probably an inevitable attack.

And then Hitler said, "Ooooh, ooh, lookie! Bad Poland! Armed! Dangerous!" And then he attacked it.

And the tanks rolled in.

Gulf of Tonkin? Pretty much the same thing: In 1964, President Lyndon Johnson claimed that North Vietnamese forces in the Gulf of Tonkin attacked American destroyers, twice . . . which wasn't true, as such, but it was a handy pretext for jumping into the Vietnam War with our best dancing boots on.

I have heard a legend—a rumor.

In 2002 the Defense Science Board proposed forming a group of American superheroes called P2OGs—an acronym for "Proactive, Preemptive Operations Group." These hundred-man teams of elite special forces and intelligence agents would operate exclusively in the "black world," financed by the CIA (and, some say, the Vatican and the Mafia), with the mandate of creating incidents that cause chaos and destabilize regions.

From a *Los Angeles Times* article by William M. Arkin:

> Among other things, this body would launch secret operations aimed at "stimulating reactions" among terrorists and states possessing weapons of mass

> destruction—that is, for instance, prodding terrorist cells into action and exposing themselves to "quick-response" attacks by U.S. forces.
>
> Such tactics would hold "states/sub-state actors accountable" and "signal to harboring states that their sovereignty will be at risk."

For example, brave and excellent P2OGs might hang around the Strait of Hormuz, loitering somewhere between Oman and Iran, on, say, an Iranian speedboat. And they might threaten one of our battleships over the radio. For fun. While speaking in an Iranian accent.

It's kind of like "Smear the Queer," where we throw the football at, say, Iran, and then everyone in the whole NATO alliance tries to tackle it.

You think that's sinister? You think that the "free press" should intervene by shining the antiseptic light of observation onto these dank matters?

OK, here's a great craft idea.

Want to prevent a rerun of the Gulf of Tonkin off the coast of Iran? *Tip off the paparazzi that Miley Cyrus is sunbathing topless at various strategic locations around the Gulf of Oman.* Then there would be no shortage of photos and YouTube videos, and far less confusion about what's going on over there.

Just send Britney Spears to the Strait of Hormuz and drop her on the frigate USS *Ingraham*. The "free press" will follow.

The United States' vital interest in uninterrupted access to Gulf oil should align itself with the United

States' prurient interest in uninterrupted access to Britney's oiled gulf. Two bad tastes that taste great together. Some things want more witnesses, some things want less around the monopolized *MEDIUS©* shrines of News Corporation. That's thinking out of the box. That's strategic coherence.

"Oh, no, please, don't bomb Iran," you whimper.

America *installed* the shah in the early 1950s and taught his security force how to *torture people*. And how did Iran pay us back? They overthrew the shah in 1979 and took a bunch of American hostages! They wanted to nationalize their oil! But it wasn't their oil anymore; it was British Petroleum's oil! They stole it fair and square, just like we just stole the oil under Iraq!

Iran's central bank issued a new banknote recently that includes a nuclear symbol: electrons flying around a nucleus, on a map of Iran.

What do you think that means? That they now have nationalized dry-cleaning but picked the wrong clip art?

MEDIUS©, god of the militainment informational complex, in his incarnate earthly form as the *Wall Street Journal*, recently told us that the wily Muscovite, Vladimir (a.k.a. "Vlad the Impugner") Putin, before stepping down (but not really stepping down), "delivered more than $700 million worth of air-defense systems to help protect Iran's nuclear enrichment and research sites from attack." Because, Vlad told al-Jazeera, "We don't think Iran should feel itself encircled by enemies."

You think you've seen defense spending? You think you've seen a muscular foreign policy?

I am going to build a motherfucking electric immigration fence around *space*.

Because, let's face it, anything short of a Final Solution constitutes a failure of will to enact a Final Solution.

If you're too limp a general public to embrace nonstop genocide, then America is neither fish nor foul—neither democracy nor empire—and it's no more possible to be both than it is to be both a Filipino drag queen and the archbishop of Canterbury.

You are only hurting *yourselves* by not supporting constant genocide.

Charles de Gaulle flunked this driver's test with the Algerians. Faced with the intersection between good and evil, he just couldn't bring himself to plow right into the pedestrians with everything he had. Too nice a guy. Too lovely a human being.

Loser.

Britain, too, feebed out after WWII when it came to really slamming the balls of the world into the lunch box of total control. They listed over into hapless, soft-fingered, crème-filled, butter-bun fagdom. And for what? Does anyone *love* them? No!

I AM NOT WORRIED ABOUT WHAT ANYONE THINKS.

IT IS MY DIVINE RIGHT TO EXPRESS MYSELF BY PERMANENTLY RUINING EVERYTHING.

I AM THE STEEL FIST OF NO TOLERANCE WHATSOEVER. I AM THE PARACLETE AND THE NOUS OF POIMANDRES TRISMEGISTUS. I WILL BOIL THE STRAITS OF HORMUZ WITH THE HEAT OF MY OWN FACE.

I WILL ENACT A FULL MASTER CLEANSE FOR THE MASTER RACE.

And that master race is ME.

It's not a global, New World Order conspiracy. It's my happening, and it's freaking me out.

I'm not inviting anyone else along for the ride. I don't discriminate. I'm like Dick Cheney, in that I hate absolutely all human beings equally, and with a lot of enthusiasm.

I store thirty-third-degree Freemasons in rubbing alcohol and use their golf shirts as moist towelettes.

The god **WARIUS©**, in his divine incarnation as the military-industrial complex, is omnipresent in every aspect of your lives—from Burger King to microchips to lightbulbs. Oil is the blood of the world. Nothing you do or own or see is untouched by its black and dripping choke-hand.

I will level with you: **WARIUS©** demands constant human sacrifices, war without end and a completely open floodgate of military spending. We all serve him. I serve him. He will kill you, or he will kill you. No corner of the world is safe. **WARIUS©** will climb through your bedroom window, shoot at your feet and scream, "Dance, bitch! Do the Lambada! I said, DO THE FORBIDDEN DANCE!"

He might kill *me* unless you serve him, and all I can tell you is, whatever you do, do *not* throw a big steaming dish of peace into that set of jaws.

Look where that got JFK, John Lennon, Mahatma Gandhi, Abraham Lincoln, Martin Luther King . . . yeah.

You get me.

WARIUS© is not someone whose shit list you want to be on.

I know him all too well.

Believe me, he makes the angry God of Abraham look like Bill Moyers.

The fact of the matter is that none of these big-picture happenings concern You People, because—really—there's not going to be enough of you left to worry about fuel consumption.

There's simply too many people alive right now.

All the neo-Malthusian techniques are going to be openly encouraged. Lobbyists will weep with joy, and so will you: I'm going to make sure cigarettes, gin and Ritalin occupy a sizable slice of the recommended daily food pyramid.

We've taken all the fun out of wars these days. Everyone is wailing and chewing the elastic out of their dirndl skirts about a little waterboarding, some stress positions.

Torture is really an inevitable part of any imbalance of power.

Mongolian hordes used to boil people alive. In my day, if you didn't send all the noses of your enemies back to their villages, or set your enemies on fire in wicker cages, you *weren't doing your job*. In 53 B.C. Mesopotamia, after Pomaxthres the Parthian violenced the hell out of General Crassus, he used the general's head as a prop during the postvictory dinner entertainment.

It's not as if humans have become any *more* civilized over time.

Want scientific proof that I am already the de facto commander in chief?

There's a treasure trove of horrible psychological experiments that have been conducted over the years that unequivocally prove, with dismaying predictability, that when someone is given the over-the-rainbow, blank-check executive super-duper powers, that only in extremely *rare cases do they* NOT BECOME CALIGULA.

And I am not just talking about Hitler, Stalin, Mussolini or the Hells Angels at Altamont.

I am talking about YOU.

Only fear of repercussion keeps you from torturing your fellow human beings—and if you are the highest authority around . . . you, too, would enjoy torturing people exactly as I do.

Psychologist Philip Zimbardo wanted to find out how captivity affects authorities and inmates, so in 1971, he turned the basement of the Stanford University Psychology Department into a mock prison.

Twenty-four male college student volunteers were divided equally into guards and prisoners for what was supposed to be a two-week role-playing simulation.

Abuses of power began on day two.

Within six days, the guards had naked prisoners hooded and down on the concrete, sitting in their own waste. And these were intellectual liberals! In California! During the Vietnam era!

Apparently it felt just perfectly natural, and nobody thought to opt out. Sure it was atrocious and demoralizing, but it must have been a deeply satisfying experience for everyone involved, because *nobody stopped.*

Guess what's even better than acting out the brutal and sadistic impulses of your own id?

Acting out someone else's.

"Just following orders."

This is to commune with *ecstacy.*

How about the Milgram experiment in 1961, during which 61 to 66 percent of participants were willing to push a button and administer increasingly painful and apparently life-threatening electroshocks to another subject (played by a screaming actor) as long as they had the encouragement of an authority figure "scientist" in a white lab coat? These hearty participants would then keep delivering up to 450 volts of electricity to the subject even after the subject had apparently *died.*

Why?

Want to shake hands with the Devil?

Look within yourself and tell me honestly that you don't want to see Cindy McCain forced to eat a live toucan.

We're exactly the same monsters that we ever were—it's just that we now pull noses off with much longer sets of tongs. Thanks to various advances in military technology, we are able to remove your nose in a way that doesn't get our actual hands as actually dirty. Perception is reality.

But really, come on. Admit it: Everyone loves a little strappado.

"I have borne [my torture] so straightforwardly that I love myself for it," said Machiavelli, after a few rounds. A good whipping really separates the Harvard men from the Yalies.

You should be afraid that your leader will torture you. Why do you think such a big deal is being made of torture these days? Why do you think this has been "exposed" in the press?

Your leaders *are dying for you to know we're torturing people*. We want you to be terrified that *you'll be next*.

It is not an empire's job to make anyone rich or happy or relieve their suffering. In fact, these things are usually most successfully achieved outside of, or in spite of, most organized social constructs. Some would argue that the best kinds of happiness happen outside acceptable limits imposed by society, law or religion—all of which are control methods that we, the Divine Few, impose on you, the Nameless Inconsequential, in the hopes that you will censor yourselves into some form of voluntary slavery (ideally, as a means of pursuing your own spiritual *virtue*).

Here's my plan: I want to kill 80 percent of the world population through the exciting use of starvation, molecular viruses, malaria, pollution and lots of dirty little wars. A select half billion of you will be chosen on the basis of health and physical attractiveness to be slaves.

Should you be lucky enough to make the cut, you won't miss the others, I assure you. Things will be a lot cleaner and more roomy around here.

Remember, as Hitler once said while discussing his plans for Poland, "Who, after all, speaks today of the annihilation of the Armenians?"

True dat.

I would like to add a final word on the important part that fashion has always played in the world of warfare.

Camo-gear can really spice up a sex life. I know my sister Drusilla always giggled uproariously when I molested her in my breastplate.

Blood and dirt on a man makes women lactate. It is the objectifying equivalent of pasties and a G-string. Throw in a javelin, and hell, you can throw in your javelin anytime you want.

Be it cheetah loincloth, Centurian shoe-shine helmet, kilt and blue body paint or simply wool beret and Molotov cocktail, the more a man looks ready to kill, the more sex he will receive. It's a simple historical fact.

I plan to increase voluntary enlistment numbers in the U.S. military by bringing back the inarguable sadomasochistic flair of Nazi tailoring.

Hugo Boss designed and/or manufactured all the fabulous outfits for the S.S. and the Hitler Youth. Why should American servicepersons be any less top-shelf?

I say shiny leather trench coats and jodhpurs

would be as much, if not more, incentive to join the armed services than university scholarships or technical training.

Who wouldn't follow Karl Lagerfeld into battle if he suddenly decided to back up his epaulets and jackboots with actual fascism?

It worked for Condoleezza, and it's always worked for the California Highway Patrol, and Tom of Finland. Bonny Prince Harry's costume-ball Gestapo uniform may have been tasteless, but surely even the persecuted among you can admit it was very fashion forward.

We need to outfit our American service personnel, and have prominent designers compete for label space on soldiers the same way they do on NASCAR drivers or bicycle teams or Olympians.

The invasion of Syria brought to you by Sean John, Baby Phat and Motorola!

Besides, designers will then be motivated to shoot war footage as their own commercials because these skirmishes will look so *sharp*.

Let's face it, one of the primary reasons anyone has ever joined the military, since the dawn of civilization, is to get laid by wearing a smart-looking uniform. If we're asking the young men and women of our lowest castes to give their lives to make the corporate elite more wealthy, then let's let them dip it in a few times before tucking them into the grass at Arlington.

Really, it's the only decent thing to do.

10

THE POLITICAL ANIMAL MUST EAT ITSELF: PARANOIA, CANNIBALISM AND EXISTENTIAL ANGST

In the councils of government, we must guard
against the acquisition of unwarranted influence,
whether sought or unsought, by the military-
industrial complex. The potential for the disastrous
rise of misplaced power exists and will persist.
—President Dwight D. Eisenhower's
farewell address

The only way to teach these people is to kill them.
—David Mamet, *American Buffalo*

This constant search for new spectacle will lead
to the destruction of the human species
as the ultimate reality TV show.
—Jean Baudrillard, *The Illusion of the End*

The trees are in misery, and the birds are in misery.
I don't think they sing. They just screech in

pain. Taking a close look at what's around us,
there is some sort of harmony: it's the harmony of
overwhelming and collective murder.
—Werner Herzog, in the documentary
Burden of Dreams

Your next president will inherit a horrible job: the lifelong enmity of anyone named Muhammad, light sweet crude heading toward $150 a barrel, and a Justice Department that will doubtless continue to investigate itself in connection to ongoing investigations of itself.

When the dust has settled, and Blackwater has finally secured the White House for me, and all rogue elements and agitators are properly dispatched and processed into the proper airports and stadiums, I am going to take a cue from KBR and Halliburton and build my very own Neverland Ranch in Dubai.

I will really do it up, Liberace-style.

I will hold my victory press conference atop Dubai's highest helipad and ride in via crane, sitting inside a nonoperational Lucite F-22. Once I "land," I will leap out of the $339-million faux-warfighter in a cloud of pink smoke, roll back the capelike sleeves on my empress-chinchilla body armor, and reveal 8-karat blood-diamond tennis bracelets stacked up to each elbow. Then, I will blow kisses to my fans and supporters: "Your tax dollars bought these, America. Thank you . . . Oh, and by the way: *nanny nanny nanny* goat, Henry Waxman (D-California), you puckered old killjoy. House Committee on Oversight and Government Reform *this*."

Then I will turn around, pull down my Lagerfeld Kevlar man-capris and show the cameras my strategically placed new tattoos—THUG LIFE beside a portrait tattoo of Henry Kissinger. The Souza march will kick in, and topless Bollywood stars will carry out a large yellow cake shaped like the Persian Gulf, featuring two delicious marzipan representations of the USS *Dwight D. Eisenhower* and the USS *John C. Stennis*, hand-sculpted by Rachael Ray.

But not on top of the cake for *any particular reason*. They don't *mean* anything. They're just a pretty, soft, decorative touch, over there next to Oman.

Anyway, after the cake, David Blaine will plummet to his death into a $140 barrel of OPEC crude, and DARPA will make Paul McCartney's ex-wife instantly grow her leg back. It will be great.

At the VIP after-party, there will be a pickled midget in every Louis Vuitton schwag bag.

And that is where the fun will end, pretty much.

Absolute power is a great gig for a while. It's a really nice greasy surge of referent power with unspeakable perks. But it's is a gig that is *guaranteed to make you barking insane, hyperparanoid and starved for the flesh of human infants*.

When you recognize no authority higher than yourself—when neither men nor gods hold sway over you—when your own moral compass is *all you have* as a guiding principle, the thing starts spinning like a motherfucking ceiling fan and anything seems reasonable, even pulling a train on your great-grandmama.

Frodo throws the Ring of Power in the volcano because he's the star of a *fairy tale and he's a FAIRY*.

Nobody *ever* throws the Ring of Power into the fiery lava unless someone pries their cold, dead, stumpy fingers off of it. Because unless you're something more or less than human, *the Ring is CRACK. It will always, always, always swallow your soul.*

You'd all be horrified and amazed at the criminal tendencies you have, if you were only given an opportunity to realize them.

WHICH IS EXACTLY WHY YOU WILL NEVER, EVER BE GIVEN AN OPPORTUNITY TO REALIZE THEM. NOT ON MY WATCH.

Free will is the enemy, which is why I am selflessly taking it away from you.

I'll let you in on a little secret: Nobody really wants to wipe out tyranny and oppression. What everyone really wants is to delude themselves that they'd be *better at it.* They'd be "benevolent dictators." But they, too, would become tyrants, just like those nice kids at Stanford. They, too, would unleash their psychotic id all over their captive subjects with no restraint whatsoever. It is a perfectly American impulse: Only tyranny is total freedom!

However, when you've finally coldcocked all your competition into Ye Olde Scorpion Hut and you're on the throne, everyone is *instantly* out to get you. The mob will be only too happy to pull your extremities out of your torso like a barbecued chicken if they catch you walking around without your usual phalanx of Secret Servicepersons.

And that's when the pounding black sweat begins.

The absolute certainty that the surveillance gnats, airborne anthrax nanobots, suicide-eunuchs and robotic spider-whippets have been dispatched to bring you low.

But I am constantly alert. I never sleep. I have lasered off all my body hair. I swallow live white mice and bathe exclusively in Pine-Sol.

Ever since Romulus killed his brother Remus in a struggle for power and founded Rome on the virtues of treachery and fratricide, "nattering nabobs," as Spiro Agnew once called them, have always looked with envy and vengeance on the president and his cabinet and wanted to Broast them slowly over a burning limousine.

Don't kid yourself—the vibe in the Oval Office has *always* been redolent of the supposedly unhinged Nixon years. It's not so much the constant assassination attempts as the fielding of nonstop black magic voodoo curses.

Did you just see a giant Krupp armor manta ray with beady red laser-eyes wrapped around George Washington's head like a tricornered hat?

I thought I did.

All American presidents stagger around the hallways shouting obscenities at the portraits on the wall. We are usually crashing from binges.

Sometimes we fall into fits of incoherence and throw obscenity-laced tantrums.

And why is this?

Leaders are *always* blamed, reviled and scapegoated for the sins of the ungovernable organisms responsible for getting them into power. They are either voted out of office in a hail of televised invective, or, in many historical cases, they are assassinated.

Add to this mélange galloping paranoia and a fizzy frisson of nuclear codes, and you can bet things have always been pretty interesting in the White House. It's like being trapped in a submarine full of burning polecats.

Nobody loves you when you're at the top. Nobody!

I warn you all: I have seen what happens when empires turn to red gravel. After we were sacked in Rome in 410, the world went dark for a thousand years. Don't think it can't happen again.

Complain about your crumbling infrastructure and overzealous Homeland Security all you like, but at least you have a system that *theoretically provides both*, which is a damn sight better for national morale than *knowing you don't*, and that at any moment some Aramis-drenched Visigoth could climb in the window of your bedroom, unzip your torso like a garment bag and eat out your liver with a crab fork.

You never know what kind of gooned-out, savage zealots are going to climb over your walls. There are inbred Scots in Nova Scotia with *three kidneys*.

You honestly think they're *not* trying to become a master race?

Tell me, what the hell else are you going to do in a wasteland like Labrador than tattoo your own face with ballpoint ink and plot to invade Michigan?

Power is *a nightmare*. When too much attention is focused on *anyone* for too long, they become *gravely ill*.

At a certain point, the Flaming Eye of Collective

Attention stares you to the point of radioactive critical mass . . . and you *blow up*.

It's like psychic *Ebola*.

Just like in ancient Greece, our cultural mythology still demands that people who fall prey to hubris must have carpet tacks stomped every half an inch all over their entire surface area.

"He whom the Gods destroy, they first make mad."

It happens to the best of us. It happens to ALL of us. It's INEVITABLE. Shit, cure DEATH, then figure that one out.

All stars eventually burn out. Entropy perverts them into the opposite of radiance—they collapse from their own gravitational weight and begin inexhaustibly sucking, sucking, sucking, inside out and backward into a blot of darker blackness, sucking everything near into a non-hole of inescapable, collapsed singular non-being.

By the time I come up for reelection, I simply won't exist anymore, but, fortunately, neither will anything else, since everything will have fallen into the inexorable pull of my own vacuum.

And it's ALL YOUR FAULT.

But know this, ye live and cureless bacteria of civil unrest: *Assassinations only prepare the ground for more ruthless and emotionally disturbed successors*.

Julius Caesar got shanked by the senate on the Ides of March, 44 B.C., which just proves you have no idea who your friends are. (And yeah, maybe I wasn't as cockeyed as you think for packing the senate chamber with my favorite horses, huh? Did you think of *that*?)

Big fucking deal—Rome still had an absolute dictatorship . . . and later they got ME.

Then the senate bribed the Praetorian Guard to murder *me*. They popped me in a hallway, and the Guard looted the palace.

But that didn't do Rome any good either.

Those bitches eventually got *Nero*, who loved to burn down whole neighborhoods and dress up in wild animal skins and attack the genitals of people tied to stakes, and who kept an Egyptian "glutton" for the entertainment value of watching him cook and eat people whole.

Nero got iced, finally—he was forced to stab himself before the guard did him.

Then *later still*, Rome got perhaps one of the most ridiculously fucked-up emperors in human history, Elagabalus, who regularly sacrificed children to himself and used their entrails for fortune-telling. Needless to say, this still happens in some parts of Africa, and for all you know, it happens once a year at *Yale*.

You know *nothing*. You have *no idea*. I can feel the horrible sucking beginning already. My chandeliers are wobbling from the sudden influx of hypodermic mosquitos.

The army finally snabbed Elagabalus. They poured molten gold in his eyes and dragged his corpse around with meat hooks.

This still happens.

Mussolini was so loathed he was eventually hung upside down by meat hooks outside a gas station so people could throw rocks at his body.

First one becomes Lord of the Flies, then one

becomes Supreme Overlord of the Flies. Finally, the Flies take over. That's empire, kids.

Not like this has ever been any real disincentive for future tyrants.

Just so you know? Right now? My tile floors are absolutely *alive* with a wiggling black lawn of robo-calamari.

Nobody even *remembers* rulers who are wimpy and just. History best remembers the psychopaths who kill high volumes of people in new and ever-more obscene ways.

Idi Amin fed his enemies' heads to crocodiles. My uncle Tiberius cut people's ears off and fed them to lions. In their quests to protect their people from the scourge of capitalism, Mao killed over forty million Chinese and Stalin killed twenty million Russians. We *all* enjoyed watching tortures and feeding people to leopards. This, like slavery and genocide, is an absolutely natural expression of ruling-class privilege.

This is *high drama*.

This. Is. Tyranny!

And I do it better than anyone else. Ever.

Should we have all tried harder to be philosopher-kings? No. Corruption is as inescapable as the sway of advertising.

Human extinction is the ultimate coliseum spectacle. In a dog-eat-dog world, man, too, must eat himself.

The meek shall only inherit the earth after we've cut down and sold every last tree and drop of water and buried so much nuclear waste that brownfields cover 91 percent of all continents and everyone gets cancer by the time they're ten.

Your government is a force of nature that wants to kill you, just like all the other forces of nature.

Any of you who have tried to stop a buffalo stampede, or an avalanche, or a forest fire, or a hurricane or a tidal wave know exactly what I am talking about. At a certain point, the thing is too fucking big to really do anything about, and you just have to step back and rely on the catastrophe's own momentum to carry it over a cliff, or burn itself out or roll it back to the great sewer of Neptune.

And you must be prepared to look down upon it from the vantage point of your $339 million air-yacht, and write off everything and everyone that ends up being a casualty of the organism's chosen path.

Am I crazy? *Or am I the sanest despot you know?*

Or am I a collapsed gravitational vortex?

How could any intelligent superhuman being in my divine position think otherwise?

How could you possibly trust someone to wield as much power as the American presidency and *not* openly share my worldview? Because I'll tell you flat out, if your president isn't up-front about it like I am, *the only thing he isn't being is up-front about it.*

You'd trust one of those slick Ivy League organic yak-fuckers who act like this is a silky, civilized world and the government isn't *the very foundation upon which hell on Earth is made manifest in order to rain a vengeful and unrelenting carnage on you, the detestably weak?*

I'm not cynical; I'm realistic.

That's why I am having a fortified brick wall with

gun turrets and uranium-coated concertina wire and an electric fence built around the entire Beltway, which will automatically dog-shock the GPS/barcode implants that I am having forcibly inserted into the soft spot of your skulls at birth which will be connected to interstellar satellite tracking devices monitored by the NSA and all major international bank operations, as part of my goal of achieving full electromagnetic spectrum dominance over all known land, sea (both surface and subsurface), air, space, aerospace and the negative space that lurks behind it.

In short, I will always know how much money you owe me and where to find you.

Nothing will challenge my divine hegemony, because I will *kill everything else first.*

Thank your lucky stars you don't live in a nation where you're not really scary enough to rule your own populace unless you're a cannibal. In some parts of Africa, if you don't eat the enemy longpig, the citizens will just think you're a *girl.*

This is for your peace of mind, America, not mine. I gave up peace of mind when I started eating my own progeny.

Here's a campaign promise: I make you a solemn blood oath that when I am your divinely elected American President-Emperor, Mercury will *never go retrograde. Ever. Again.*

If Mercury continues to threaten the ongoing interests of the American people, it must prove that it can be responsible enough to exist.

Diplomatic options have been tried. But I do not

negotiate with any space that harbors evil. *Even the space between your ears.*

I am selling something even better than audacious hopes.

It's called Hopelessness. It's a place beyond reason.

Hope implies that somebody else is going to do something that makes your life tolerable. I guarantee I have no intention of doing so.

You attain hopelessness when you have finally achieved losing everything, including your mind, your soul, and your freedom. It's the most rare and special kind of freedom—the absolute freedom that comes from having no freedom whatsoever.

You will love being hopeless. The good news is, you're at least halfway there.

When you're finally beyond hope and safely in jail, toiling away for the greater good, you will see me on TV in all my golden glory, in the radiance of all my powers, in the light of my celestial moons.

And you will know this: You, your friends, your loved ones and your children are my *punks*. You've all been *punked*. You are all my little *punk-ass bitches!*

Now that, my fellow Americans, is equality.

Booyah. You've been kissed by God. Tremble before my Omnipresent Leading Brand. I AM THE HOT WHITE EYE.

My library just spontaneously shredded itself.

Now you know the truth. Now you are free to act in a manner that guarantees the removal of all freedom. You are at liberty to achieve this "liberty" beyond liberty.

For fuck's sake, don't be sad, stupid and obedient. That's why you're so detestable in the first place. All the incredible weapons you've worked so hard to pay for? *Give me good reasons to use them against you. Give me the satisfaction of denying you the medical attention I enable you to need.*

Go ahead. Make my day. Vote for me so we can share the thrill of this gypsy knife fight together: the timeless war that has always been endlessly fought between beautiful royal divinities like myself and fat, uninformed, air-sucking, drunk, pill-popping statistics like invisible, broke-dick you.

This is true intimacy. This is communion. This is your Rapture. Run, don't walk. Sing, don't cry.

Nobody really wants peace. And anyway, even if they did, I am pleased to announce that peace is finally, officially obsolete.

Mahatma Gandhi and Martin Luther King embraced a path of nonviolence and demonstrated a moral leadership that eroded the public's faith in their leaders and forced their nations to rethink the inhumane policies of their governments. But in this rootin' tootin' climate of total moral nonchalance and ethical zombism, nonviolence would be absolutely pointless!

There is no hook left in you to hang peace on—no ember of humanity's tender feelings left to blow on. The entertainment god *MEDIUS*© has rendered your soul safely blunt and extinguished.

Nowadays, you would just watch all the Indians and blacks getting wordlessly clobbered by riot cops and laugh, and laugh, and laugh like you were watching *Jackass*. And then you'd rewind it and watch it again.

You are safe now from the vain charade of salvation.

As a populace, you are immature and emotionally retarded. Your crazy-dreamer-style political decision-making is based on a totally optimistic disregard for actual politics, the learning process and logic in general.

Example: You've been absolutely knuckle-punched in the collective throat by executive power in the last six years, but you still vote from your heart instead of your brain.

But this is where the United States gets its strength.

America's greatest talent—and your only hope for competing with the stunningly self-abnegating, industrious groupthink of the Chinese—is the accidental genius that happens when spoiled Americans over-indulge themselves. Elvis. Madonna. Richard Pryor. Miles Davis. *Grand Theft Auto*. These are America's best exports: sudden bursts of louche creative expression that offend the sensibilities of all previous generations.

Americans are fat adult baby-people who would rather play Texas hold 'em than learn to calculate probabilities. But the interesting and bankable thing about Americans is that *you will eventually learn to calculate probabilities by playing Texas hold 'em*.

Sure, the wheels are coming off the country now. But all it's going to take is one insectoid, socially repellant, electrical engineering douche-water geekbag out of the thousands who graduate from MIT every year to come up with a car that runs on old circuit boards, corpses, crack vials or discarded halogen lamps—and your whole economy will boom all over again.

The Stormtroopers of the New American Police State will cramp everyone's style for a while, the same way the Transportation Security Administration has ruined travel for you—but this will make you safer in the end. What we are really doing is protecting you from yourselves. We know what can happen when you have too much freedom. Lessons have been learned. If we have to take our nightsticks and hammer every naked, filthy hippy protester into hemp butter, *antiestablishment sentiment will never, ever look "cool" again.* The sixties are in the process of being written out of history and soon will have *never happened. Go back to your bomb shelters. Pray to your Holy Presidential Emperor for protection.*

I WILL DENY IT TO YOU! I am a nuke-white galaxy of swirling wormholes!

Ironically, the last great hope of liberty and liberalism, and your only recourse if you want a barrier of civil protection against your own government, lies in the tenacious, cold-dead-claw pistol grip of the hated NRA. Libertarians and other minority-loathing rednecks, bless them, have never quite trusted their government, and have always vehemently defended their right to stockpile vast arsenals of state-of-the-art weaponry. And not just so schizophrenics can shoot schoolchildren!

These fearful patriots have been gearing up for God knows what—a dark future that might require a showdown with . . . the barbarian *Mexi-Goths.*

Or worse: the savage, blue-assed *Québécois.*

Or bevies of anarcho-syndicalist mule deer.

But, I must say, even atavistic, beer-damaged, morbidly obese, impotent, bigoted, aerosol-cheese-huffing rednecks like the ones who demonstrate weapons on the Military Channel are necessary to America. They are a crucial digestive enzyme that, like bile, is revolting by itself, but makes sense working in conjunction with everything around it.

Because they do have a point: *Quis custodiet ipsos custodes?* (Who will watch the watchers?)

I, however, am unwatchable.

Even the cyborg ninja-bats skittering between my walls have learned this. I am the Warrior Christ of the Apocalypse, returned for vengeance. And verily, the Judgment Day has come.

I pledge to avenge America against itself.

U.S. senator George Prescott Bush, grandfather of George W. Bush, was a director and shareholder of firms that profited from, and in at least one case was directly involved with, the "financial architects of Nazism," according to a 2004 article in the U.K. *Guardian*. His company assets were finally seized in 1942 under the Trading with the Enemy Act, but honestly—seriously—this is so-o-o-o not shocking.

Everybody knows that the tattoos on concentration camp victims were IBM numbers; that IG Farben—the conglomerate responsible for Bayer aspirin—manufactured Zyklon B; and that Bayer sponsored wacky quack Josef Mengele in his research performing anesthesia-free root canals on Dustin Hoffman; that the Rockefeller Foundation and the Carnegie Institute funded Nazi eugenics projects in the 1930s;

that Hitler participated in designing the slave-labor-built Volkswagen Beetle. Your very own secretary of state Breckinridge Long gave the Ford Motor Company license to make Nazi tanks. General Motors, ITT, DuPont and Chase Bank all very happily did business with the Third Reich.

Prescott Bush's money never really went away. Soon, it will all be funneled into his descendant young George Prescott Bush III, beloved son of **WARIUS©**.

Scientists have published the entire gene sequence for the 1918 influenza virus, "the deadliest pathogen in human history," making it one of the more readily available potential biological weapons of mass destruction. Frankly, I tried a similar recipe last year when *TIME* published an entire article on how to refine yellowcake uranium, and it didn't work at all—instead of ending up with my own warhead, I just got nitric acid and tributyl phosphate all over my countertop. Just *try* getting $UO_2(NO_3)_2 6H_2O$ out of your saucepans. Next time I want a nuke I'm just going to Pakistan.

WARIUS© demands more bodies. Demands, and demands, and demands. And **BLUTO©**, god of the prison-industrial underworld complex: He, too, demands more bodies.

In fact, all your state corporate gods demand more bodies.

WARIUS© thinks he can demand MY body.

But, seriously? Fuck **WARIUS©**. Shiv me once, shame on the Praetorian Guard. Shiv me twice—total destruction of everything that ever existed and all consciousness that it ever did.

WARIUS© may talk a big game, but not for nothing have I been stewing in resentment for 1,800 years. I will prove once and for all that **WARIUS©** no longer has undue influence over political agendas, foreign policy or election outcomes.

WARIUS© will finally bow to the will of CALIGULA!

I am on the way to the stealth-elevator to plunge two miles undergrond into my lead cave, to join Henry Kissinger and Miley Cyrus. I have all the nuclear launch codes stored in my satellite phone. I have bionic rottweilers that piss nerve gas and have three rows of titanium shark teeth. I have a dead-loyal bunch of absolutely ruthless, buck-naked Liberian ex–child soldiers from Charles Taylor's "Boy Brigade," armed to the tits with TDI KRISS Super V machine guns, flamethrowers, MP7A1s, .50-cal. Barrett sniper rifles, silenced High-Standard .22 assassination pistols and MP-5s, quite a handful of grenade launchers and all the meth they can smoke..

I am shredding absolutely everything, except for documents that will support my blackmailing of foreign powers.

Does a private military really think it can pull another hostile takeover on CALIGULA? Do Blackwater, Triple Canopy, Raytheon, Northrop Grumman, Lockheed Martin, EADS, Boeing, DaimlerChrysler and young George Prescott think they can fuck with me? They think they can tell ME what to do? Even WITH the ongoing and tacit complicity of the Pentagon?

I will destroy all e-mail, obviously. All of it. Everywhere. I will jam the entire world of e-communication with my horrible new space magnet.

With surgical strikes detonating miles beneath the sea I will make new hurricanes, new earthquakes, better tsunamis. I will make new coasts by cracking off the old coasts. I will take the Fifth, the Fifth, the Fifth Amendment and be unable to recall anything whatsoever, even my own divine presidency. I have stealth submarines and Rolex B-79 Combat Owls and oh, ho, I have all the nuclear codes right here in my phone, **WARIUS©**, you bloated pack of murderous, alky gargoyles, and I'll have you know that the boys over at DARPA have already built me a *very special widget add-on* that looks just like a SHINY RED BUTTON that . . . 89IKKKKKKKKKKK

KKKKKKKKKKKKKKKKKKKKKKKKKKKK
K

KKKKKKKKKKKKKKKKKKKKKKKKKKKK
KKKKKKKKKKKKKKKKKKKKKKKKKKKKKK
KKKKKKKKKKKKKKKKKKKKKKKKKKKKKK
KKKKKKKKKKKKKKKKKKKKKKKKKKKKKK
KKKKKKKKKKKKKKKKKKKKKKKKKKKKKK
KKKKKKKKKKKKKKKKKKKKKKKKKKKKKK
KKKKKKKKKKKKKKKKKKKKKKKKKKKKKK
KKKKKKKKKKKKKKKKKKKKKKKKKKKKKK
KKKKKKKKKKKKKKKKKKKKKKKKKKKKKK
KKKKKKKKKKKKKKKKKKKKKKKKKKKKKK
KKKKKKKKKKKKKKKKKKKKKKKKKKKKKK
KKKKKKKKKKKKKKKK

. . . WAIT! Hah. Just like in *Jaws*, I'm not actually *dead yet*. Now's when I come back all bloody and really

ACKNOWLEDGMENTS

No experts wanted to be affiliated with this book by name, but the authors would like to acknowledge the contributions of our anonymous constitutional law experts, and "Lieutenant Dan," a Deep Throat–style financial tipster.

POLITICAL CRONIES WHO WILL ALL ATTAIN HIGH-PAYING CZARSHIPS AND OTHER DISTINGUISHED POSITIONS OF RANK

Bill "Art Czar" Clegg, Colin "Supreme Overcommander" Dickerman, Gini "Idi Amin in a Keyboard-Print Scarf" Wilson, Steve "More Paranoid than Tiberius" Wilson, Dan Gingold, Adam Sontag, Mookyung Sohn, Mitzy and Sean McFate, Adam and Bart, Nancy Balbirer, Isabel Milenski, Rachelle Garniez, Steven Felty, Erin Simpson, actual historian James Quillin, anonymous senior defense officials, Muire Dougherty and the ASH-X (Artistes Sans Hollywood) movement.

MARKED FOR DEATH

Whoever designed the buggy, font-happy, totally unpredictable autoformatting on MS Word for Apple 2004.

INTEGRITAS!

SOURCES

Author's Note: Historians should be prevented from reading this book, and especially this list, which will be deemed incomplete and infuriating. Historians should probably be prevented, period.

Wikipedia.com*

Suetonius, *Lives of the Caesars*

Anthony A. Barrett, *Caligula: The Corruption of Power* (Yale University Press, 1989)

Albert Camus, *Caligula*

---

*Many journalistic and academic institutions pooh-pooh Wikipedia because it has user-generated content, and its information is therefore considered suspect, but much of this is a bad rap. For the most part it is pretty obvious when bad information has been added, e.g.: "**Lucius Tarquinius Superbus** (also called **Tarquin the Proud** or **Tarquin II**) was the last of the seven legendary kings of Rome, son of Tarquinius Priscus and son-in-law of Servius Tullius, the sixth king. He was of Etruscan descent and ruled between 535 BC WHEN A CHILD WAS BORN NAMED JASON SANDERSON AND HE WAS FAT FAT FAT FAT AMAZINGLY FAT AND GAY and 510 BC."

Robert Graves, *I, Claudius*

Chalmers Johnson, *Blowback* (Henry Holt, 2000), and various highly recommended Internet articles

Niccolo Machiavelli, *The Prince*

Paul Strathern, *Machiavelli in 90 Minutes* (Ivan R. Dee, 1998)

Ken Knabb, ed., *Situationist International Anthology* (Bureau of Public Secrets, 1981)

Peter York, *Dictator Style: Lifestyles of the World's Most Colorful Despots* (Chronicle Books, 2006)

Sun Tzu, *The Art of War*

Carl von Clausewitz, *On War*

Mike Huckabee, *From Hope to Higher Ground* (Center Street, 2007)

Lawrence Welk (with Bernice McGeehan), *My America, Your America* (Prentice Hall, 1976)

Guy Debord, *The Society of the Spectacle* (Rebel Press, no copyright)

Marshall McLuhan and Quentin Fiore, *The Medium is the Massage* (HardWired, 1996)

Gore Vidal, *The American* Presidency, The Real Story Series (Odonian Press, 1998)

Mark Zepezauer, *The CIA's Greatest Hits*, The Real Story Series (Odonian Press, 1994)

H. L. Mencken, *The Vintage Mencken*, gathered by Alistair Cooke (Vintage, 1955)

Arundhati Roy, *An Ordinary Person's Guide to Empire* (South End Press, 2004)

Nancy Snow, *Information War: American Propaganda, Free Speech and Opinion Control Since 9/11* (Open Media, 2003)

Joel Andreas, *Addicted to War: Why the U.S. Can't Kick Militarism* (AK Press, 2004)

Terry Deary and Martin Brown, *The Wicked History of the World: History with the Nasty Bits Left In* (Scholastic, 2006)

Terry Deary, *The Ruthless Romans*, Horrible Histories (Scholastic, 2003)

Terry Deary, *Rotten Rulers*, Horrible Histories (Scholastic, 2005)

Philip Hill, *Lacan for Beginners* (Writers and Readers, 1997)

Deborah Schnookal, ed., *One Hundred Red Hot Years: Big Moments of the 20th Century* (Ocean Press, 2003)

Russ Kick, *The Disinformation Book of Lists: Subversive Facts and Hidden Information in Rapid-Fire Format* (Disinformation, 2004)

Russ Kick, *50 Things You're Not Supposed to Know* (Disinformation, 2003)

Stanford Encyclopedia of Philosophy, "Aristotle's Political Theory"

The Economist (many, many issues)

HARPER'S (many, many issues)

Foreign Affairs (not as many issues)

Various Seymour Hersh articles in the *New Yorker*

Dana Milbank's "Washington Sketch" column in the *Washington Post*

Harvey C. Mansfield, Jr., "Returning to the Founders: The Debate on the Constitution," *The New Criterion* 12 (1993)

Jason Leopold, props for asking the right questions

DOCUMENTARIES

ENRON: The Smartest Guys in the Room
The Corporation
The American President (PBS series)
National Geographic specials:
  Air Force One
  Inside American Power
  Guns, Germs & Steel
The American Ruling Class
Various PBS *Frontline* investigations

WEB SITES THAT PROVIDED SOMETHING THOUGHT-PROVOKING

Truthout.org
CommonDreams.org
Freedom and Reason (Andrew Austin—wwsword.blogspot.com)
PopulistAmerica.com
HistoryChannel.com (forums)
DefenseTech.org
TomPaine.com
321gold.com
dollarsandsense.org
thecloud.crimethinc.com
CriticalResistance.org
GlobalResearch.ca
Pbs.org (*Frontline*)
FreedomofthePress.net
Mondediplo.com

Birdflubook.com
TheAtlantic.com
Smokershistory.com
Bartleby.com
Indybay.org
Fas.org

INFLUXES OF PASSIVE INFORMATION/INFLUENCE

The NewsHour with Jim Lehrer
Democracy Now!
Countdown with Keith Olbermann (MSNBC)
The Rachel Maddow Show (Air America)
Military Channel (a nonstop background drone of explosions)

A NOTE ON THE AUTHOR

Author/culture critic Cintra Wilson regularly writes the "Critical Shopper" column for the *New York Times*. Her books include the seminal *A Massive Swelling: Celebrity Re-Examined as a Grotesque, Crippling Disease* and the acclaimed novel *Colors Insulting to Nature*. As a journalist, she has been a perennial contributor to Salon.com, and has appeared in a great many glossy magazines, newspapers and literary journals. Her regular political column, "The Dregulator," can be accessed at www.cintrawilson.com. She lives in New York City.